Anonymous

Laura Erle

Vol. I

Anonymous

Laura Erle
Vol. I

ISBN/EAN: 9783337052164

Printed in Europe, USA, Canada, Australia, Japan

Cover: Foto ©ninafisch / pixelio.de

More available books at **www.hansebooks.com**

LAURA ERLE.

A Novel.

BY THE AUTHOR OF
'BLANCHE SEYMOUR,' 'ERMA'S ENGAGEMENT,'
ETC.

IN THREE VOLUMES.

VOL. I.

LONDON:
TINSLEY BROTHERS, 8 CATHERINE ST. STRAND.
1873.
[*The right of translation and reproduction is reserved.*]

LAURA ERLE.

CHAPTER I.

'Claude! You come to-day? I did not expect you till to-morrow!' exclaimed Mrs. Elliott, who, having settled in her own mind that her nephew would not arrive till Friday, felt naturally annoyed with him for appearing on Thursday.

'Yes, aunt Eleanor, I am come,' returned the gentleman, who always resented his relative's plans in his behalf. 'Is there any reason why I should not come to-day?'

'No, my dear; only I had fixed in my own mind that you would not come till to-morrow.'

'The delightful thing is that you are come, dear Claude!' cried his sister Audrey, springing up joyfully to welcome him.

He returned her greeting warmly, bestowed a frigid kiss on the tip of Mrs. Elliott's ear, which she presented to him for the purpose—she always meant to present her cheek, but failed, chiefly because she disliked equally kissing and being kissed—and continued:

'Harold Carew is coming here for a few days, aunt Eleanor. He wants to see Farleigh Abbey, and can go from here more easily than from Oaklands, where his mother is staying. I have asked Digby Forester to come here too, after the funeral on Wednesday. It is so wretched for him alone at Glynton.'

He made the communication as one who knows that his news will be badly received, and who is anxious to get it over.

'You continue the family tradition of making Enleigh a refuge for the destitute,' said the lady sarcastically. 'We live on the early Christian principle, that nothing we have is our own. I only hope that when we fail some of the many we have ruined ourselves for will be willing to receive us into their habitations.'

'Entertaining Harold Carew and Digby Forester for a week is not likely to hasten our ruin,' retorted Claude, who never could be persuaded that 'silence is golden.'

Mrs. Elliott may be shortly described as the hair-shirt of the Dashwood family, and admirably did she fulfil her function of mortifying its members.

She was not really Claude's aunt, though he and his brother and sister always addressed her as such. She was a cousin of their father's, who had, ever since their mother's death, lived at Enleigh House, where she exercised despotic sway. There had been some early 'love passages' between her and the handsome cousin, Charles Dashwood, whose children she afterwards watched over with a mother's care, though without a mother's tenderness; but he had forsaken her for a beautiful Irish girl, and the fact deepened the natural prejudice entertained by her against Ireland and the Irish. The young Dashwoods suffered keenly from this prejudice. They loved their mother's country and compatriots as intensely as Mrs.

Elliott hated them, taking every reflection on the land or its inhabitants as a personal insult; while the lady, with that exquisite courtesy which distinguishes a certain type of Englishwoman, made a point of attributing to the young people who were unfortunate enough to share a nationality she disliked all the faults and vices supposed to be characteristic of the Irish race, as a whole.

She assumed that they must be untruthful, untidy, quarrelsome, and so given to reckless hospitality as to be always ready to waste their substance in riotous living.

Claude's communication brought down a storm of sarcastic invective on his head; for besides her bitter prejudice against Ireland and the Irish, Mrs. Elliott had also a prejudice against matrimony, and the object of her life seemed to be to keep Audrey from entering the holy estate.

She had already made her refuse two good offers, for no reason that any one could discover; and she heard of the approaching visit of two young men with about as much pleasure as a careful shepherd would feel on receiving from a pair of respectable wolves an offer to look in and inspect his flock. She deeply regretted her inability to prevent such an incursion; but Charlie Dashwood, who now reigned at Enleigh in his father's stead, had given his brother *carte blanche* to invite any one there whom he pleased, during his own enforced absence abroad on account of his wife's health; he would, besides, have resented anything like want of hospitality towards an old friend and neighbour, such as Sir Digby Forester was.

But though Mrs. Elliott could not prevent the visit, she could make it a visitation to Claude and Audrey at least, and she did so by anticipation now. She left nothing unsaid that could wound their susceptibilities. Her wonderful insight into character enabled her to 'read each wound, each weakness, clear;' she could thus give little stabs and thrusts, in all sorts of skilful ways, into her unfortunate victims' very tenderest parts. Her friends were, in her eyes, so many pincushions, designed by Providence to receive the pins and needles which it was a necessity of her nature to emit from time to time. A whole shower of these pleasing weapons was now poured forth on Claude and Audrey. First, they were reproached with their Celtic blood; this reproach always brought on a passage of arms between her and Claude, who would deny vehemently that he shared one drop of that obnoxious mixture,—his 'dear mother being,' he averred, 'of Norman, not Celtic origin.' Next the lady animadverted severely on their Anglican tendencies—the form their Irish hankering after Rome took—thereby showing her appreciation of the Protestantism of the sister country; and she proceeded then to reflect on their Irish accent, which consisted chiefly in aspirating the 'h's' in their *whats, whens,* and suchlike words.

Claude bore it as long as it was in the power of masculine nature to bear without swearing, and when this point was reached left the room. He was followed speedily by Audrey, who joined him on the lawn, where he was standing by the railing, a gloomy frown on his face. Her own bore the 'badgered' expression it always assumed during an action with Mrs. Elliott.

'Hasn't that woman the most confounded temper!' was his exclamation as she came up. 'How long has this fit lasted?'

'It has only just come on. She was an angel till she heard about Digby; and how could you invite Harold Carew here, Claude? He and she will fight incessantly.'

'I couldn't get out of it; he all but asked to come. Charlie told him to run down whenever he liked, and he is crazy to see the abbey.'

'Where did you meet Digby Forester?'

'He called on me. He is awfully cut-up about his father's death. It happened at Athens, and all the arrangements about the funeral have been most painful to him. It is to take place at Glynton on Wednesday.'

'Is he much changed? He has been away five years.'

'He looked awfully ill, I thought; though

he is burned as brown as a berry, and you never saw such a beard as he has! Of course I couldn't do otherwise than ask him here.'

No Dashwood ever could do otherwise than ask every one to Enleigh on every possible occasion.

'I don't know which is worse—the profound dulness when we are alone, or the dread of quarrels when any one is here,' sighed Audrey.

Both stood looking gloomily straight out before them, heedless of the sun setting gloriously and of the beauty which lay all around, like people whose lives are dimmed, not by any great calamity, but by constantly-recurring petty annoyances, which quell the buoyancy of the spirit, and from which there is no prospect of escape. The brother and sister bore a strong resemblance to each other. Both were tall and singularly graceful, moving with the free firm tread indicative of perfect physical development. Audrey was eight or nine years younger than Claude, being at this time only nineteen. Her masses of black hair were drawn back from her forehead, and coiled in thick plaits round her head. Her large soft gray eyes looked almost black too, under their long dark lashes; ordinarily she had not much colour, but exercise or excitement would bring the blood mantling to her cheeks.

'How is Laura?' asked Claude, after they had stood in silence for some time.

'Very well—the only bright thing about the place. She is going to have a Gregorian choir, and is full of it. I think it is dismal myself; at present we give utterance to a prolonged howl; but she says it is all as it should be, and that it will save her a world of trouble.'

'Let us go down and see her.'

They turned towards the Rectory, and at the gate met Laura Erle,—'the only bright thing about the place,'—a tall slight girl, with a graceful bending figure, laughing dark eyes, a brilliant complexion, and a sweet mobile mouth, round which smiles seemed always dimpling.

At the first glimpse of her the cloud on Claude's face disappeared.

'Well, Laura!' he exclaimed, with that unconscious change in his voice by which some men always acknowledge the presence of a woman not nearly connected with them. He held her hand for a second or two, looking at her with a softened expression. 'How are you? It seems an age since I have seen you! I hear you have a Gregorian choir; but how about the ladies? that isn't orthodox.'

'I know it; and it has exercised me terribly.'

'Couldn't you get rid of them?'

She shook her head.

'Banish my girls? that would never do! Besides, if I did, they would betake themselves to Little Bethel in a body, carrying their mankind with them; such is the depravity of woman! And where should I be then? I should be left a melancholy example of what may result from too close an adherence to mediæval precedent in this nineteenth century.'

'And how have you been?' repeated Claude. 'Working yourself to death, as usual?'

She shook her head gaily.

'I am in rude health, as you may perceive.'

'Laura, Harold Carew is coming to Enleigh,' said Audrey impressively. 'Isn't it appalling to think how he and aunt Eleanor will quarrel?'

'Harold Carew! Who is he?'

'I thought I told you about him. He is the greatest curiosity extant—a determined *célibataire*, and a *célibataire* who thinks every woman who sees him wants to capture him.'

'A *célibataire!*' returned Laura, with a peculiar intonation, indicative of complete incredulity, on the word. 'How I shall enjoy seeing him! I always like to look at those natural phenomena.'

'The ladies all detest him,' said Claude, in the tone of a man who flatters himself that they don't detest him.

'That is a mistake; they should convert

him,' responded Laura, who looked capable at that moment of converting any number of *célibataires.*

'He has a pleasing little peculiarity of assuming that women have no souls,' explained Audrey; 'the assumption pleases him and doesn't hurt me; and I admit that he amuses me excessively, he is so pedantic and so priggish, and so altogether satisfied with himself.'

'Isn't he afraid of you?'

'Very much so; but curiosity to know what the talking pink-and-white thing will say overcomes his fear. They call him Harold Harefoot, because he runs away from the ladies; but the name drives him wild, for he says "Harefoot" has nothing to do with running away, and means something quite different. His mother, Lady Emily, is the dearest old woman; and it really is the most amusing thing to hear her talk of him. She worships him, and is as anxious to impress his perfections on all the world as if she had some suspicion of how much he is disliked.'

'It is a real misfortune to a young man when his mother insists on enrolling him in the Corps of Irresistibles,' observed Miss Erle philosophically.

'There is some more news for you,' said Claude; 'the Ellises have taken Oaklands, and Farleigh Abbey has been bought by a tallow-chandler!'

'A tallow-chandler! Shade of S. Bernard!' ejaculated Laura.

'Perhaps I ought rather to say a wax-chandler. He has made fabulous sums by inventing and patenting the Only Original Inodorous, Unspluttering, Inexhaustible, and Inextinguishable Wax-dip for the Million.'

'I hope he won't restore and—ruin the abbey.'

'Carew hopes so too; but he anticipates the worst, and the object of his visit is to see the place before the work of destruction is begun.'

'Who did you say had taken Oaklands?'

'The Ellises.'

'Such horrid people, Laura,' remarked

Audrey; 'the girls so fast, with fly-away heads, and talking such slang that I can hardly understand them.'

'Uncommonly pretty Violet Ellis is, though,' said Claude.

'Pretty! What do men call pretty? She hasn't an idea in her face!'

'One doesn't always want ideas in a woman,' responded Mr. Dashwood.

'That is lucky, for in Violet Ellis, at least, you couldn't get them.'

'Then you know them, Audrey?' asked Laura.

'A little. I have met them occasionally, but I dislike them and their whole set.'

'Well, you are not likely to see much of them; Oaklands is seven miles off,' observed Claude.

CHAPTER II.

It had been a question how Mrs. Elliott would receive Sir Digby Forester. To the great relief of Claude and Audrey she was gracious. Perhaps his face, which bore distinctly enough the traces of his grief—he had lately lost his father—touched her.

'You must make yourself at home, and do exactly as you please,' she said to him. 'We shall be quite alone, with the exception of Harold Carew, who is coming here next week. Do you know him?'

'Yes; he and I are old allies.'

'Well, I hope you like him. I can't say I do; but that is a matter of taste.'

Sir Digby and Audrey had known each other well in former years, and now resumed, as if by instinct, the old habit of calling each other by their Christian names; though during his absence Audrey had grown from a somewhat wild girl into a beautiful and rather stately young lady.

It was no fancy on her part that he grew more cheerful as they recalled together old scenes and days. His face would brighten wonderfully as he took his place beside her. That Mrs. Elliott allowed her to enjoy his society uninterruptedly was a constant source of surprise to her. As a rule, that lady saw in every man a devouring wolf, from whose fangs it behoved her to rescue her lamb; and this had gone on for so long that Audrey accepted it as the order of nature, and never thought of asserting her right to a share in any wolf whatsoever. Wolves were for other people— not for her. But Mrs. Elliott showed no disposition to interpose between her and Digby. Perhaps it was that even she could not associate anything wolfish with one so gentle and winning. Whatever may have been the cause, she read quietly in one corner of the room; Claude lay on a sofa, absorbed in the paper, in another; while the young man and the lady exchanged confidences to their mutual content.

Mr. Carew's arrival was a disagreeable interruption to this state of things. He set up all Mrs. Elliott's bristles; and when they were set up they rubbed and irritated every one.

The main object of his visit was to inspect Farleigh Abbey, the lion *par excellence* of the neighbourhood, which had lately been bought by an eccentric millionaire, about whose oddities and peculiarities innumerable stories were circulated.

Mr. Carew, who considered the abbey of national importance, heard of the purchase with great disgust. Believing all the current stories about the new proprietor, he was already lamenting, by anticipation, the approaching ruin of one of the finest ecclesiastical buildings of the kind in England. Hence his anxiety to see it before the work of destruction should be complete.

But to do so was a matter of no little difficulty. Mrs. Elliott always had a plan, and her plans were always made with reference to some deep scheme which she had matured in her own brain, and towards the accomplishment of which she strove to make every event tend. As she kept her schemes absolutely to herself till they were ripe for execution, no one could see the object of the wonderful projects she at times unfolded, or understand her systematic opposition to any proposal which did not emanate from herself. So resolute was this opposition, that, without coming to an open rupture, it was impossible to carry out anything she disliked.

Mr. Carew wished to go over to Farleigh with Claude or Digby; but Mrs. Elliott had no intention of allowing him to do anything of the sort. She had resolved that the whole party should go. It was a good opportunity for calling on the De Montmorency family, and she would not miss it.

It was vain to oppose her; Claude stormed, but he invariably ended by doing as she wished; so they were to go in a body, the latter gentleman indemnifying himself by getting his sister to ask Laura Erle to accompany them.

'She can ride the gray,' he observed.

Mrs. Elliott heard of the invitation with deep anger. One of her plans was to keep Claude and Laura apart. She was strongly of opinion that they saw decidedly more of each other than was good for either.

'I wonder you are always asking Laura to ride with you, Audrey,' she remarked, in a voice suggestive of cantharides; 'as she is never likely to have even a donkey of her own to go about on, it seems but doubtful kindness to accustom her to thoroughbred horses.'

'She doesn't often ride with us, aunt Eleanor, and she works so hard that a change occasionally does her good.'

'Oh, of course; and as she, no doubt, means to catch Claude, I daresay she thinks it wise to begin by catching his horse.'

Audrey would bear patiently any number of aspersions on herself, but the least attack on her friend made her put on all her war paint.

'I won't listen to such remarks, aunt Eleanor; you ought to be ashamed of making them;' and she left the room.

The lady next attacked Claude.

'So I hear Laura is going to favour us with her company to-day. In my time young women waited till they were asked, but now a different fashion prevails.'

'I asked her to come,' said he boldly.

She laughed scornfully.

'It used to be said, "In vain the snare is set in the sight of any bird," but now the birds are such fools that they jump, like "doting mallards," into the trap set openly before their very eyes.'

This stab was given merely to relieve the irritation of Mrs. Elliott's feelings. She was too shrewd a judge of character not to be well aware that Laura Erle was incapable of setting a trap for Claude. She might fall in love with him, 'like a romantic fool'—that was the lady's own comment—she would never try to 'catch him.'

'Where is your eccentric guest, Claude?

I want to see him,' asked Laura, as she stood on the steps, all brightness and animation.

'He is keeping out of your way. He was terribly alarmed when he heard you were coming, though I told him you were harmless.'

'I wish he would show. I want to see what a determined *célibataire* is like.'

Her curiosity was gratified. As she was running up-stairs to her friend's boudoir, she and Mr. Carew came upon each other with such force that both were nearly knocked off their feet.

'I beg your pardon,' said Laura instinctively; and then, prompted by her youth and the spirit of fun in her, 'Don't be alarmed; I am quite harmless.'

The gentleman muttered something not very intelligible and stood stock-still, gazing in utter amazement at the bright-eyed, laughing vision before him.

He was tall and dark; his glossy black hair very much and very smoothly brushed backed from an exceedingly clever, keen, hairless face, with a rather sarcastic expression.

In her surprise Laura had dropped her habit, which got twisted round her feet so that she could not move; neither could she stoop to free it without again falling foul of the stranger.

'I must ask you to move a little,' she said, 'or I cannot get up my habit.'

He almost sprang to the other side of the wide staircase, whence he deliberately watched her as though she had been a wild animal whose ways he was studying.

'I'm harmless, unless I'm stared at too much; that irritates even the mildest creatures,' she went on, embarrassed by this inspection, from which she was unable to escape, as her habit had now got caught in the ornamental iron-work of the banister, and she had some difficulty in disentangling it. '"You are requested not to irritate the animals," is always written up in the Zoological Gardens. Now you have looked at me, perhaps you would kindly go away.'

'Oh, certainly,' still gazing fatuously at her. 'Where can I go?'

'Wherever you were going when you nearly knocked me down.'

'I couldn't help it; you came in my way.'

'You came in mine.'

'I didn't see you.'

'So I suppose; if you had you would probably have run the other way.'

Mr. Carew took this as an allusion to his sobriquet of Harefoot, and flushed to the roots of his hair. He did not like being ridiculed by this bright-faced damsel, who looked up mockingly at him from under her long lashes. Owing to the retention of her habit, she was unable to stand upright, and her crouching posture may have added piquancy to the laughter which lurked round her dimpled mouth.

'I should have done no such thing,' he retorted. 'I should not have altered my course in the least.'

'Wouldn't you have got out of my way? You don't hold, then, that manners make the man?' interrogatively.

He flung back his head angrily; went down a few steps and then came back again. 'Can I do anything to help you?' in a doubtful voice.

In the interval Miss Erle had freed her garment, and now stood facing him in an upright attitude.

'You have timed your offer so admirably that I am enabled to decline it, with thanks;' and, bowing, she ran up-stairs.

Mr. Carew looked after her with a glance compounded of anger and surprise. He was still in the hall when she came down again. Involuntarily their eyes met, and Laura, to whom everything served as a pretext for merriment, could not help laughing. He did not feel equally disposed for mirth. Annoyed and angry, he met the young lady's amused glance with one of stern reprobation.

Sparkling all over with laughter she burst into the drawing-room.

'I've seen Dryasdust!' she exclaimed. 'He exceeds even your description, Audrey,' and she related her adventure. 'He has a nice face, though,' she concluded. 'I like it.'

Harold, through the open window, heard the laughter and merry voices, not quite without a suspicion that he may himself have been the subject under discussion. He thought he caught the word 'Harefoot,' and was sure he heard 'Dryasdust.' It may be explained that he had distinguished himself highly in a number of literary 'ologies.' He was an archæologist and a paleologist and an ecclesiologist, et cætera, and was generally accepted by his friends as an undoubted authority on architectural and other kindred topics.

'So I hear you had an encounter with Miss Erle,' said Sir Digby to him afterwards.

'Miss Erle was it? I met a termagant who nearly knocked me over, and then vituperated me for getting in her way.'

The baronet laughed.

'She is not likely to suffer pain and grief, like the Psalmist, from keeping over silence, I must say,' he remarked reflectively.

'What a termagant!' ejaculated Mr. Carew.

'You should hear her touch up Claude Dashwood, as she does sometimes, in first-rate style.'

'She would touch up the devil himself,' with acerbity. 'Is Claude Dashwood going to marry her?'

'It is not improbable.'

'Good God! Conceive being tied for life to a woman with a tongue like that!'

CHAPTER III.

As long as the oldest inhabitant of ——shire could remember, Farleigh Abbey had been the favourite resort of holiday-makers, picnic-parties, and pleasure-seekers in general.

It was an old historic place, where ecclesiologists and archæologists met and talked in a learned way pleasing to themselves; where they fought and dined and mutually admired each other, looking down on their neighbours because their neighbours called Farleigh an abbey, while they affirmed that it was a priory. The neighbours had vague ideas on the subject of clerestories, too; confounded the refectories with the dormitories; and showed themselves generally ignorant of things Benedictine and Cistercian.

But ignorance of technical details is by no means preventive of very real enjoyment, and in some unscientific, sentimental way 'the abbey' embodied many poetic ideas, and was productive of much pleasure of a not unworthy kind to the simple town and country folk. It was, besides, a source of prosperity to the provincial metropolis, for visitors from many lands, and of various race and speech, came to gratify there their pilgrim-hunger.

Harold Carew, being what he was, was naturally on fire to bring his architectural knowledge to bear on it. He had not been in that part of the country before, and felt, in some sort, personally wronged that there should be an abbey which he had not inspected.

Not that he called it an abbey. He had no words strong enough to denounce the ignorance of the common vulgar, or the wilful disregard of truth shown by the better informed, who persisted in transferring to a priory the dignity and designation of an abbey.

It may be frankly admitted that it was not a pleasant thing to visit an abbey, or, indeed, any architectural or historical lion, in Mr. Carew's company, if there happened to be any one present inclined to respect the traditions of the place.

He was a very mountain of uninteresting but detestably real learning, which he was always burning to pour forth for the benefit of his hearers and the demolition of their most cherished beliefs.

Claude and Audrey looked forward with no little uneasiness to the call they were about to make with him. He had put up all Mrs. Elliott's bristles in the morning by throwing doubts on the antiquity of some oak-carving at Enleigh. That favoured abode was famed —in the estimation of its possessors—for its oak-staircase, its oak-floors, its oak-carving. Its oak enabled it to hold its own with the abbey as a local lion, and the lady could not but feel aggrieved at any reflection on its genuineness. There had been a rather sharp skirmish between her and the visitor on the subject, but out of deference to urgent remonstrances from Claude and Audrey, she had promised to say no more about it, and during the drive maintained an elaborate silence; while the gentleman descanted indignantly on the ignorance displayed by people in general about such things. He animadverted further, in strong terms, on the sin of speaking of Farleigh as an abbey.

Mrs. Elliott's silence had the effect of irritating him more than any positive contradiction. All his remarks were aimed at her —he assumed that she upheld the abbatial designation—and his combativeness was such that the refusal of the enemy 'to come on' only increased his ardour for the fray.

Providence, in its infinite goodness, soon provided him with a foe as ready to fight as he was.

Claude and Laura had ridden on, but not wishing to reach Farleigh first, had waited for the carriage at the foot of a steep hill, which always necessitated a slackened pace. When it overtook them, they continued to ride beside it, and Mrs. Elliott formally introduced Harold to Laura. He raised his hat with as low a bow as his sitting posture enabled him to accomplish.

'Mr. Carew and I have met before,' said Miss Erle, her face dimpling all over with smiles at the recollection of their first encounter.

Mr. Carew was not quick at saying nothing. He always wished, when he talked, to talk sense, and he was, at that moment, unable to think of a single suitable remark consistent with strict veracity. He could not say he regretted having nearly knocked her down. He did not regret it; he felt that it had been her doing as much as his; so he took off his hat a second time, bowed, if possible, lower than before, and resumed his animadversions on the want of accuracy displayed by the people of ——shire on the subject of the abbey.

Audrey and Digby had listened to these in discreet silence, only offering such harmless observations from time to time as would suffice to show a decorous attention, anxious, above all things, to prevent a collision between the speaker and Mrs. Elliott.

But Miss Erle was by no means disposed to be thus quiescent. She had a word for every one, and would, with the greatest imaginable readiness, have discussed with the Chancellor of the Exchequer the best method of reducing the income-tax. She was, besides, enthusiastically fond of her native county, and not at all inclined to hear it vilified in silence.

'Every one in ——shire who knows anything knows that Farleigh is a priory, not an abbey!' she exclaimed; 'though, of course, no one thinks of exhibiting his knowledge on his sleeve, as if it were something very unusual.'

Mr. Carew's face was a study. The delight of finding an antagonist who would fight struggled with intense astonishment at the nature of that antagonist, and at the audacity which could thus challenge him, as it were, to single combat. Even clever men were somewhat wary how they entered the lists with him, yet this provocative-looking impersonation of impertinence seemed to have no more hesitation in contradicting him than if he had been a baby of five years old.

After gazing at her for a second or two in silence — these various feelings depicted on his countenance — he answered in his most sarcastic tones:

'Then if they know it, it makes the case all the worse. There is some excuse for ignorance; there can be none for a wilful misrepresentation of facts.'

'It has nothing to do with a misrepresentation of facts,' retorted Laura. 'It is a mere *façon de parler*. Besides, Farleigh Abbey sounds much nicer than Farleigh Priory. I shouldn't know the dear old place if it was called the Priory. A priory is a rubbishy kind of thing! There's a priory at Hillingdon, where the four old Miss Pringles live—all with corkscrew curls and thin lips and such scraggy necks!'

This style of argument quite overcame Mr. Carew. What had the childish fancy that an abbey sounded 'nicer' than a priory to do with facts?

'I don't know about a priory being a rubbishy kind of thing' (in a tone of lofty contempt), 'but the priory at Hillingdon, which is a real priory' (cuttingly), 'is one of the most valuable Benedictine remains in England.'

'Is it? Then the Miss Pringles are *analogues* with it. They are valuable remains too.'

Every one laughed except the gentleman addressed. Even had he had a spark of humour in him, the subject was in his eyes too serious to admit of light treatment.

'You consider the matter a fitting one to hang jests upon? You are quite right. I always make a point of jesting on subjects I don't understand.'

This was the severest thing he could think of at the moment.

'Indeed!' rejoined his antagonist, in a tone of well-feigned surprise. 'I confess, if you had not said so yourself, I should not have thought you given to jesting.'

A glance of contempt mingled with reprobation, and then—' As a rule I endeavour not to speak on subjects I don't understand.'

'You are so right; but exceptions prove the rule, don't they? And your remarks about our ignorance are the exception in this case. Had you understood us better, you would have seen on what very insufficient grounds you were condemning us.'

Mr. Carew did not address another word to Miss Erle during the rest of the drive, but he watched her with a look of mingled curiosity and aversion, till his attention was attracted by the flag floating from the abbey tower, announcing that the new proprietor was in residence. The contempt which, quite unconsciously, he entertained for the *nouveaux riches* was on the present occasion increased by an indefinable feeling of annoyance that Mr. de Montmorency should be enabled by his riches to become possessed of such an historic monument as Farleigh. As long as it had remained in the hands of a family as old and respectable as itself, he experienced no shadow of jealousy. Time had hallowed their claim to it; besides, they would respect every stone of it as scrupulously as they did their own escutcheon. They held it, as it were, in trust for the nation, and felt their responsibilities as guardians of such a treasure.

But these upstart millionaires who had now stepped into it would be for ever demonstrating their right of possession by changes and adaptations to modern wants which would entirely destroy the historic and architectural value of the building. He felt a sense of personal injury at the transfer of the abbey to such people, and the sight of the flag increased the anger he felt.

Royalty was entitled to a flag, and great ducal or lordly houses might legitimately display such a symbol of distinction; but a tallow-chandler, who never had a grandfather, probably not even a father! Mr. Carew's not very captivating countenance assumed a more than usually sardonic expression as the carriage stopped at the abbey door; an expression that did not augur well for the harmony of the visit should he and the new proprietor meet.

They did meet; and as he was as anxious to show the abbey as Harold was to see it, they were not long in coming to an understanding, and the whole party started to 'do' it.

It was famous not only for its architectural beauties but for its historical associations. Kings, queens, statesmen, and other celebrities, had at various periods sojourned there; and the bedrooms and tables and chairs and counterpanes used by them had all become historical and legendary and renowned and mouldy.

Mrs. de Montmorency had not been long enough in possession to find the office of cicerone altogether one of pleasure. She felt awed by the number, rank, and reputation of the mighty men and women who had made her home famous. Of some of them she had never even heard till the auspicious day which made her mistress of the abbey. Two titles were especially puzzling—Henry Chichele's Tower and the Venerable Bede's Turret.

A gifted being, who had the whole history of the place at her fingers' ends, condescended to act as housekeeper under her, and the obvious course on this occasion would have been to get her to show the guests round.

But greatness has its penalties. Such a course would have been not only incongruous but humiliating. It would not do to let people fancy she was ignorant, or unable to master the details connected with the traditions of the house. In truth, the courage she displayed in this matter was beyond all praise, for she never started to 'do' the abbey without secret trepidation.

On this especial afternoon she was more than commonly uneasy. Something in Mr. Carew's manner made her nervous.

Mr. de Montmorency was ostentatious in pointing out the changes he had made and contemplated making. To be just, these changes were only such as were absolutely necessary to render the place comfortably habitable; but hearing of them was a sore exercise of Mr. Carew's self-control.

Every stone of the old part of the building was, properly enough, sacred in his eyes, and his alarm and anger were extreme and justifiable on perceiving that Mr. de Montmorency attached as much value to the restorations effected by the late owner as to the really genuine remains.

But this want of discrimination resulted merely from ignorance, not from any wilful disregard of the relative merits of the respective work; and in spite of his somewhat childish determination to assert his rights by pulling down and building up as he pleased, it was easy to see that in reality he wished to preserve carefully all that was worth preserving in the beautiful pile of which he had become the possessor. He only wanted a little judicious educating; but to be judicious was not in Harold Carew's nature, and the marvel is that one stone of the abbey remained upon another after his visit. He 'rubbed' the tenacious, sensitive, and irascible proprietor the wrong way at every step; pooh-poohing openly the modern restorations and additions, and going into architectural raptures over the older parts. The effect was naturally (human nature being weak) to make Mr. de Montmorency undervalue the latter, not from any want of artistic feeling, but out of pure contradiction, and merely for the sake of asserting himself, and pronounce the former authoritatively the only portions worth attention.

This so stimulated Harold's combativeness that the course through the abbey, or round it, was a pilgrimage of danger; but the first explosion was caused by an historical, not an architectural, blunder.

Laura had not gone three yards with Mrs. de Montmorency before she took her measure, so to speak, and proceeded to 'draw' her for the edification of her friends; she did it so naturally that none but her intimates perceived that her questions were not put in good faith. Audrey and Claude were convulsed with laughter, and the former in vain made signs to her companion to desist; but Miss Erle's love of fun was irrepressible, and she went on unheeding, eliciting from her hostess the most delicious mistakes and misstatements. Mr. de Montmorency believed intensely in his wife and in her learning, always listening with profound respect to her historical expositions.

'Whose room is this, Mrs. de Montmorency?' asked Laura, as they went through a ghostly apartment, hung with blue.

'This is Queen Eleanor's Parlour, but it has been turned into a bedroom, and you see the curtains are embroidered with Eleanor crosses in honour of her. She worked that counterpane herself, as a gift to the rebel Simon de Montfort.'

'Indeed! How ungrateful of him to have become a rebel!'

'This room is full of rebellious reminiscences,' said Mr. de Montmorency, laughing immensely at the conceit. 'That is Oliver Cromwell's prie-dieu chair,' in a tone between pride and shame.

Like a loyal subject he detested Oliver Cromwell; still, as the Protector's sojourn at the abbey had evidently added to its celebrity, he did not like to condemn him too severely.

Harold Carew uttered a low growl. To hear Simon de Montfort and Oliver Cromwell stigmatised as rebels, the memorials of whose presence had to be apologised for, was almost more than he could bear. There had been many premonitory symptoms of a storm, and it was doubtful how long he would retain even the outward semblance of calm.

'Where does this lead to?' asked Laura, as they went up a dark winding stair.

Here was the most trying part of Mrs. de Montmorency's work. Henry Chichele had proved too much for the united historic lore of the family. This staircase led to his tower, and she always feared some crucial question, her inability to answer which would betray her ignorance. The painful thing was, that all her friends would keep on asking who he was. She concluded at last, so ignorant did every one seem about him, that he was some local celebrity—a highwayman, perhaps, whose story she would one day learn. Meantime she put a bold face on the matter.

'This is the Venerable Chichele's Turret,' she replied with an assured air, though secretly so nervous that she was not the least aware what words were coming from her lips.

'The Venerable Chichele! Dear me! Who was he?' asked Miss Laura; while Harold, standing close by, looked unutterable scorn.

'No, no, mother; you are making a mistake,' said her son; 'this is Henry Chichele's Tower.'

'O, to be sure! I always forget,' with the nervous laugh peculiar to her on such occasions, and putting her hand up as if to hide her face. 'Henry Chichele's Tower. The Venerable Bede's Turret is higher up.'

'And who was Henry Chichele?' repeated Laura.

'Bæda!' exclaimed Harold; 'he never was here!'

'Indeed he was,' returned the hostess

quickly, delighted to parry the question about her stumbling-block, Chichele. 'We are going up to his turret now. It is very curious, and there are two holes in the floor worn by his knees. He was such a good man that he was always saying his prayers!'

'Is that the test of a good man?' said Digby, laughing.

'Good or bad, he was never here—he cannot have been,' returned Harold.

'Never here, sir! never here! What the deuce do you mean?' cried the host, turning sharply on the speaker, his face perceptibly redder.

'I mean that Bæda never was here.'

'Peter, sir! Peter! Who is talking of Peter?' stammered the gentleman angrily. In his excitement he had mistaken the name. 'We are talking of Bede—the Venerable Bede —who certainly was here. This is his turret, always so called; and there are the marks, sir, of his knees, sir; holes made by him from his unceasing prayers.'

'Whoever or whatever made the holes, he

didn't,' repeated Harold scornfully. 'It is incredible how people pervert facts. Bæda—'

'Bæda! Bæda! Who was Bæda? I am speaking of Bede—the Venerable Bede,' angrily.

'Well, Bede, the Venerable Bede, if you like it better. I say he never was here, never had a turret here, and never said his prayers here.'

'What, sir? how, sir?' stammered Mr. de Montmorency, scarcely able to articulate from sudden anger. 'You come here, a perfect stranger, and deny well-known facts! How can you tell who has been here or who has not?'

'I can tell, as every one can who has the least knowledge on the subject, that Bæda, or Bede, as you corrupt his name—'

'Corrupt his name! What the deuce do you mean? I corrupt the name of one of the chief historical characters of my house!'

'I say that Bæda, or Bede, if you prefer to call him so,' went on Harold, unheeding, 'can never have been here, because not one stone of the building was laid at the time of his death;' and he proceeded with a learned lecture on Bede first and then on Farleigh Abbey, or Priory, as he maintained it to be, scouting the idea that the former could ever have visited the latter.

He stamped his foot contemptuously on the indentations popularly supposed to be the result of the recluse's continuous genuflexions, denouncing indignantly the credulity and ignorance which could believe in them, totally regardless of the feelings of the unfortunate Claude, who, having brought him there, felt answerable for his conduct.

Words are quite inadequate to describe Mr. de Montmorency's sensations, his looks or gestures during the delivery of this harangue. His face grew redder and redder, till there seemed serious reason for apprehending a fit of apoplexy; he gesticulated furiously, endeavouring to refute his adversary, but vainly, for rage completely stopped his articulation, and his efforts ended in abortive spasms of attempted enunciation.

At length he found words—all except the h's, which he could not possibly stop to supply at such a crisis—and fired a broadside into his enemy.

Who was Mr. Carew, that he came there to upset the associations of the abbey? He—Mr. de Montmorency—had paid for it and its traditions in hard cash, and was not going to see them disputed by 'an itinerant—an itinerant—seeker after some new thing,' ended the enraged proprietor, at a loss for a peroration.

The astonished and dismayed assistants could only stand by in helpless silence. Interference was useless, both the disputants being too angry to listen to any voice save that of their own passion. But when Mr. de Montmorency had somewhat relieved his feelings, his wife and son on one side, and Claude and Digby on the other, tried to stop the combat.

Whether they would have succeeded or not is doubtful, but Laura created an effectual diversion; for just as the combatants, like two enraged African travellers, were about to rush on each other again, she addressed Harold in her clear fresh voice,

'Mr. Carew, as you have effectually destroyed my belief in the Venerable Bede ever having been here, you are bound to supply a satisfactory solution of the great hole question. What made the holes? Mind, you must give a romantic reason for them.'

He turned on her savagely. 'Argument is useless with a person who sees matter for jesting in everything.'

'It is equally useless with one bent on believing in traditions for which he has paid in hard cash,' she returned with sudden gravity, and lowering her voice so that he alone could hear it. 'I wonder you don't see that, and that it is highly inexpedient to quarrel on the subject here. Of course, no one seriously believes such rubbish.'

He stared at her in blank amazement. 'Inexpedient! Quarrel!' Never before had such words been addressed to him.

Silent from sheer surprise, he did not utter one syllable when Mr. de Montmorency, disregarding all remonstrance, returned to the charge.

The whole party quitted the Venerable Bede's Turret in a state of most uncomfortable excitement, and all oppressed with a vague sense of guilt, save the two combatants.

They continued to eye each other like dogs who have been forcibly separated while fighting. Harold glared too from time to time at Laura, as does the dog at the master whose authority prevents his renewing the attack.

Fortunately there was no more to see indoors, and the fresh air tended to calm their feelings. The walk was concluded with only one more explosion on Harold's part, and that a mild one comparatively, for he addressed his remarks chiefly to Laura, making them the vehicles for some very cutting sarcasms on herself.

Miss Erle gave him, it must be admitted, as much as he gave her, and when they went in to tea it would not be easy to say with whom he was most indignant, her or Mr. de Montmorency.

CHAPTER IV.

This tea had sorely exercised Mrs. de Montmorency, and the visitors had been unwilling listeners to a little colloquy on the subject, which caused them to look forward to it with no small anticipation of amusement.

It appeared that, the family dinner hour being six, the head of the household could not be brought to see the necessity of a meal an hour or an hour and half only before that great event in his day.

'Tea, my dear!' the visitors heard him exclaim, evidently in answer to some remark made to him by his wife; 'why, it is just dinner-time! What do people want with tea at this hour?'

'No one dines so early as we do, and people always have tea at this time; Plantagenet and Gwendoline will tell you so.'

Plantagenet and Gwendoline were the offspring of Mr. and Mrs. de Montmorency.

'Bosh, my dear, bosh! Six o'clock isn't early. I won't have such waste as tea at this time of day.'

'It looks so odd not to have it. It is so inhospitable. Plantagenet and Gwendoline always say—'

'There, for God's sake, my dear, don't tell me what Planny and Gwen say. Ask the people to stay to dinner if they are hungry—though, no, don't; for then Planny will want me to have out my best sherry.'

'Tea is ordered, mother,' said Plantagenet, to end the matter.

He had drawn near during the colloquy, suspecting its nature.

'Ordered, ordered!' said Mr. de Montmorency irascibly. 'I'm not allowed to be master in my own 'ouse—not in my own 'ouse!' In moments of excitement he always omitted his h's. 'Then I won't have plates of bread-and-butter cut and wasted. Let them cut for themselves if they want it. What a party to feed!' he muttered; 'all as hungry as hawks. Three great he-men, and one, two, three women! The old one will go into the cream like bricks, and even the young ones drink tea now like fishes. I say, Planny,' in a loud whisper, 'don't order any cream, there's a good boy—milk will do.'

'All right,' responded Plantagenet, nodding his head as if quite entering into the paternal feelings on the subject of cream.

This conversation was carried on so audibly that the 'people' could not choose but hear, with what exquisite amusement may be conceived.

It would have been heroic to decline tea; but human nature, it cannot be too often repeated, is weak, and so many and such excellent stories were circulated in the countryside respecting the way in which the inventor of the Great Inextinguishable Dip emulated Harpagon, that curiosity to see him preside at his own board, even if that board was spread only for five-o'clock tea, overcame every other consideration. Besides, the hostess so pressed them, that they had no choice in the matter.

On going into the library, where tea was prepared, Mr. de Montmorency cast a reproachful glance at his son.

There were two silver cream-jugs on the table, besides a jug of milk. For one brief moment a hope that all three contained only the less expensive fluid buoyed up his mind; but no, there was no mistaking the yellowish liquid, all destined to be consumed by that omnivorous party.

A plate with about four or six small slices of bread-and-butter represented the edible portion of the repast.

The host sat down, anxiously surveying every drop of tea poured out. He would not have touched anything himself to save his life; nor did any of his family venture on sharing the obnoxious meal.

Plantagenet, on seeing the scanty supply of bread-and-butter, rang the bell.

'Now, Planny, what do you want?' exclaimed his father, with an instant prevision of farther expenditure.

'They haven't brought bread-and-butter enough.'

'Why, what do you mean? There's a whole plateful.'

But even as he spoke it had disappeared, Gwendoline having distributed it amongst the company.

'O, well, it's gone!' in a dismayed tone; 'but you needn't have any more. The ladies are helped, and I daresay you gentlemen don't care for thin slices of bread-and-butter?'

The gentlemen unanimously repudiated such a taste.

'Never mind—nothing,' said Mr. de Montmorency eagerly, the moment the servant appeared.

'Yes, yes, some more bread-and-butter,' cried Plantagenet and his mother simultaneously.

'Very well, then; but bring the loaf—don't cut it. D'ye hear, Thomas?' raising his voice; 'bring the loaf. You fellows are so wasteful, cutting whole plates full of bread-and-butter which is never eaten. I don't grudge anything to any one, but I hate waste,' this last to the company, who uttered a decorous assent to so admirable a sentiment.

Harold Carew was too superior to be amused; but the less transcendental members of the party had much difficulty in maintaining a becoming gravity. The state of affairs did, however, at last dawn upon that austere champion of truth, and he took a grim revenge on the proprietor of the Venerable Bede's Turret by consuming all the bread-and-butter which Thomas, in defiance of his master's orders, brought in cut—a proceeding which subsequently elicited from Mr. de Montmorency the somewhat coarse remark that 'more valuable things went into Mr. Carew's mouth than ever came out of it.'

The Farleigh dinner-bell was ringing as the visitors drove away. Their host, apprehensive that he would be called on to entertain them at that meal, had indeed sped their departure with rather unseemly haste.

'Why, it's six o'clock, close upon; you will be very late. What time do you dine?'

Assuring him that they would be home in ample time, they took their leave; and, in spite of the turret episode, both visitors and visited were mutually pleased, and parted hoping they would soon meet again.

Mr. de Montmorency was the only exception to the general satisfaction.

'Unfaith in aught is want of faith in all;'

and Harold Carew's conduct had disgusted him with the whole party.

'Ill-conditioned, ignorant brute!' he exclaimed, alluding to him as the carriage drove off. 'Why you should have given them tea, Gwen!' going back to the library. 'Don't let that cream be thrown away—that is if there is any left,' looking anxiously into the cream-jug. 'A set of idle people come here to make domiciliary visits—'

'Domiciliary stuff! They came to call.'

'To make domiciliary visits, I say; and not satisfied with hearing me abused in my own house, you order up whole plates full of bread-and-butter and tea enough for a regiment. I'll stake my existence that Plantagenet's whole company wouldn't eat as much in a month as that long-legged ugly-looking brute did at one sitting.'

'If they didn't, they would become small by degrees and beautifully less,' returned Plantagenet, laughing.

'It's all very well for you to laugh, sir. You would laugh the other side of your mouth if you had to pay the bills. I'll never have one of that party inside my house again; mind that, Gwen. Confound it, I don't keep a hotel! That long-legged ass says I oughtn't to touch the west window. I'll block it up altogether! I'll have it done to-morrow; I'll give orders about it to-night. He says every stone of it ought to be looked on as sacred. I'll have every stone broken up to make the new road to the brick-kiln. I will, I'm hanged if I don't! And cream the price it is! I offered them milk, hoping to save the cream; but Planny, with his officiousness, pressed the cream on them. Do you know what it is a pint, sir? The brutes had moustaches too!'

'Mr. Carew hadn't,' said Mrs. de Montmorency, seizing with avidity on any extenuating circumstance.

'Because he hadn't manhood enough in him to grow one,' retorted the gentleman, determined not to be mollified; and he proceeded to say that he would give half a crown apiece for every hair Mr. Carew grew on his face. 'A ton of bear's grease wouldn't make that fellow grow a moustache; and yet he comes here giving his opinion about my house and my doings, and says people never lived here who lived and died here, as all the world knows. I'll block that window up. I will, I will!'

The exciting incidents of the visit to Farleigh, and the culminating episode of Mr. Carew's consumption of the bread-and-butter, and the consequent discomfiture of the eccentric proprietor of the Venerable Bede's Turret, so transported Mrs. Elliott that she forgot all her ill-humour of the morning, and was as genial, bright, and charming as she could be at times. She was so lovable in her *good* fits that she made every one forget how intensely disagreeable she could be in her bad ones. So entirely had she got over her annoyance, that she insisted on keeping Laura to dinner in order to 'talk over' the visit.

Laura and Mrs. Elliott together, when both were amused and in good spirits, were, as Audrey expressed it, 'better than any play.' They drew each other out, and vied with each other in the quaintness and absurdity of their remarks and criticisms. Even Harold Carew was observed to smile grimly once or twice during dinner that evening.

He was still full of the deepest resentment against Laura; language failed him to stigmatise her flippancy, her presumption, her abominable propensity to thrust herself into conversation with every one. But she stimulated his curiosity. Of all the specimens of the incomprehensible sex he had ever come across, she was the most remarkable, and his eyes followed her every movement with an intentness not unobserved by Mrs. Elliott, in whose active brain a new scheme began to acquire consistency.

Audrey, Claude, and Digby all volunteered to walk home with Laura. The Rectory was close to Enleigh, the way leading through the gardens and shrubbery. The whole party stood on the steps for a few moments, breathing in the freshness after the day's heat. The dew lay heavy on leaf and flower; the air was rich with the scent of roses and magnolia blossoms. They were all talking and laughing together except Harold Carew, who stood apart, still casting moody glances at Laura, round whom Claude was carefully wrapping a red cloak, she protesting the while that she did not need it, and that he was stifling her. They started; but she, seeing that Harold was not coming with them, turned back.

'Won't you say good-night to me, Mr. Carew? As we have quarrelled all day, we ought to shake hands at parting, oughtn't we?' holding out hers, and looking up at him from under her hat, which was tilted low down over her eyes.

'Good-night,' he said, in a voice which betrayed unconsciously the irritation and antagonism she aroused in him, and touching her hand much as he would have touched some obnoxious animal.

He felt annoyed with himself because he could not help being angry with her. Why should he let such a chattering compound of volatility and presumption disturb his equanimity?

'You mustn't think us quite depraved, even though we do call Farleigh an abbey,' she said, with a laughing light in her dark eyes.

He muttered something ungraciously; her phraseology provoked him inexpressibly. Why did she use such exaggerated terms? Depravity had nothing to do with the matter. He had not said they were depraved; only inaccurate or ignorant.

'He is a bear, you will admit,' was Laura's laughing comment as she rejoined Claude.

'Then why trouble yourself about him?' he returned a little impatiently.

She glanced at him from under her long lashes.

'Because, most mighty, I did not wish to show myself a bear too.'

On their return, Digby and Audrey stood for a few minutes together on the steps. A star shot across the sky, traversing in a moment millions of miles, and disappearing behind the woods faster than the eye could follow it. A white owl flew between them and the moon, looking ghostly, somehow, in the gleaming light. His discordant 'tu-whoo' made Audrey start and shiver. There is something weird and suggestive of coming ill in the note. It broke in on her dream.

'I can't bear the owl's cry,' she said shivering; 'it always frightens me. Let us go in.'

In the hall they found Mrs. Elliott looking over a basket of visiting cards.

'I see Mrs. Ellis and Lady Emily Carew called to-day, Audrey. We must return their visit in a day or two.'

Audrey knew that this was inevitable, much as she dreaded an intimacy with the family at Oaklands. She had no sympathy with any member of it, and especially disliked one of the girls, Violet, from a suspicion she entertained that Mrs. Elliott meant her—fast, modish, and 'loud'—to displace her beautiful, but, alas! impecunious, friend Laura in Claude's heart.

CHAPTER V.

AUDREY always felt helpless before Mrs. Elliott's resolves. That lady had a will of iron, and had never been known to swerve from a purpose she once set before her. Yet Audrey was not without hope that her brother might be saved from Violet Ellis, her aunt notwithstanding. She could not conceive a worse fate for him than to have her for a wife. To Miss Dashwood, refined and fastidious, nothing could be more abhorrent than Violet's fastness, her slang, her unswerving devotion to one object—that, namely, of getting a husband at all costs. To obtain this worthy end she was ready to sell herself to the highest bidder with shameless indifference.

Claude was fastidious in his views about women and in his requirements in a wife, and it was on this fastidiousness his sister relied, hoping it would counteract the force of the battery his aunt might bring to bear on him.

It is true he had frequently expressed much admiration for Violet; but it seemed to Audrey that no man who took pleasure in Laura's society—as he evidently did—could also take pleasure in Violet's.

No two girls could be more entirely different. In a worldly point of view Laura was heavily weighted in the race. She had absolutely nothing but her own merits to recommend her—her brightness, her ready wit, and generous heart. She was literally penniless; one—*horrendum dictu*—of fourteen children. There had been sixteen; but a beneficent Providence had, in its infinite goodness, seen fit to withdraw two—boys, of course—from a quiver which, even after their departure, could not but be deemed sufficiently full.

Of the fourteen living children, nine were of that sex which the world contemns while finding it indispensable.

Mr. Erle, the rector of Smedston, had exactly three hundred and twenty-five pounds a year, and no hope of anything more, on which to feed, clothe, and educate this portentous family; to live like a gentleman, and to keep up many parish charities.

Was it wonderful that his nightly thoughts troubled him? That, as girl after girl made her appearance on this mortal scene, he asked himself in ever-deepening despair, 'What is to become of her?' Some irrepressible, but of course unpardonable, doubts as to the absolute abominableness of female infanticide would at these seasons of depression present themselves to his mind, doubts which, as became a good Christian and a gentleman, he crushed back steadfastly, exorcising them as devices of the enemy, and resuming patiently his increased burden. He reminded himself that hope is one of the cardinal virtues; he therefore hoped much—sometimes even against hope. These hopes centred chiefly in his eldest son, John— to send whom to Oxford the Rectory family had denied themselves more than they ever cared to speak of—and in his daughters, who, he trusted, would marry.

The descent of some half-dozen heaven-directed husbands was the only solution of the many difficulties surrounding his path which Mr. Erle could see. He did not pause much to reflect whence these husbands might come. He concluded girls had a knack of picking up husbands somehow; if his did not, God help them! They must starve. At this point in his reflections Mr. Erle would bury his face in his hands and groan aloud; and then his wife, who had no need to ask what was troubling him, would speak some words of hope and consolation. Her hopes and beliefs centred in her son John. She was less sanguine than her head about those heaven-directed husbands, who, poor fellows, were anticipated less in their character of loving and cherishing than of endowing with all their worldly goods.

Mrs. Erle was beyond the age of illusions. She knew that young men with goods to bestow have no need to go into the byways of life to seek maidens to endow withal. They can stand in the market-place, and crowds will flock to be hired. Therefore she was not sanguine as to that matrimonial panacea, the thought of which afforded so much balm to her helpmate's soul. Laura might marry. The mother could not understand how any man could look at her bright-haired, bright-faced darling without loving her; for Laura was the light not only of her father's but of her mother's life—dear to her as her child first of all, then as her friend, her adviser, and comforter, whose tender sympathy, ready help, and practical good sense never failed.

But Mrs. Erle had stared reality too closely in the face not to know that Laura might not be able to marry a rich man, and she had suffered too much herself as the impecunious mother of a large family to wish to see her daughter the wife of a poor one. A keen pang would shoot through her heart when she thought of her girls' future—a tight feeling of anguish worse than any bodily pain.

She feared and felt especially for Laura. Was she to see this tender bright creature fade and wither, cut off by the bitter circumstances of her lot from all the hopes and joys of happier girls?

Of course thoughts of Claude Dashwood did from time to time force themselves on Mrs. Erle's mind, but she resolutely put them away; and without actually saying it in so many words, she tried to make Laura conscious that a match between her and the rich, handsome, young patrician at the great house —second son though he was—was the least likely event in the world to happen. The frequent intercourse with Enleigh, though it had its advantages, was indeed a source of no little anxiety to the mother. The men Laura met there—and they constituted her whole society—spoiled her for any less finished specimens of the sex. How could she, accustomed to the style, conversation, and attention of these gay young favourites of Fortune, content herself with the untravelled, unpolished country clergyman, say, who would be alone likely to seek her hand? She would always be trying him by some aristocratic standard. He might exceed in real worth every one by whom she measured him; it is, however, a melancholy fact that real worth cannot always hold its own against ease of manner and that indefinable something which marks the man who has seen the world and mixed in society.

Claude was always at the Rectory. Every day, so long as he was at Enleigh, he would come with a book, or a paper, or a flower; anything served for an excuse. He would take Laura away to play croquet or to ride or walk; and Mrs. Erle, knowing what a hard life the girl had, acting as governess to her brothers and sisters, teaching in the schools, visiting in the village, superintending the choir, had not the heart to deprive her of the change and brightness his presence brought her. Besides, the intimacy had gone on so long that it would be difficult to break it off without assigning some definite reason for doing so, and that might compromise Laura.

It was not possible to conceive a greater contrast to Miss Erle in every way than Violet Ellis.

The Ellises were wealthy, and not scrupulous where it was a question of securing a rich husband.

Violet was the fourth of six daughters, the three eldest of whom had, at the opening of this story, been 'out' for some time; but though they had toiled laboriously all day, and all night too, they had hitherto taken nothing. It was hard work, and the poor souls were weary enough of being exposed season after season in the market-place, in hopes of finding a purchaser who never came. The eldest girl, Margaret, showed her sense and self-respect by going 'in' again; but Violet, in all the pride of eighteen, thought this a tame conclusion, and resolved to play her cards differently. She would avoid 'failure'—there is parliamentary authority for that admirably just and appropriate expression—at all hazards; she was therefore, as Audrey felt, a dangerous rival to Laura, who, not looking on 'failure' as absolutely the greatest of earthly misfortunes, had some scruples left, old-fashioned it may be, but respectable, as to the means to be used for insuring 'success.'

CHAPTER VI.

'Are you coming with us to Oaklands, Claude?' asked Mrs. Elliott, the day she had settled to go there.

'To Oaklands? Yes, I don't mind going. I have nothing to do here. Is Laura going?' turning to his sister.

'No. I said nothing about it; she is so busy.'

'Busy! Nonsense! That girl is worked to death. She looked so pale and worn this morning! The drive will do her good. I'll go over to the Rectory and make her come.'

Mrs. Elliott began urging a host of objections, but Claude would not stay to listen.

'I sha'n't keep you; she is never a minute getting ready.'

He met the object of his search at the Rectory door, equipped for walking.

'That is all right, Laura. I came to look for you; we are going to Oaklands to call. Come with us.'

'I should like it of all things; but I'm going out with papa.'

'Never mind; you can go with him another day. It is too hot to walk.'

'It is hot, and I should like to come immensely; but, you see, I couldn't leave papa,' deprecatingly. 'Thanks, so many, all the same.'

'You must come, Laura. I'll tell Mr. Erle—'

'Not for the world,' putting out a detaining hand. 'I wouldn't leave him this afternoon on any account. He has to go a long way over the hill, and he feels the walk less when he has a companion.'

'Let Amy go,' said Claude, his face darkening as it always did at the least opposition to anything he proposed.

'It is too hot for her.'

'It seems to me that all the work which is too hard or too disagreeable for other people is put on you.'

'Well, quite right. I'm the strong one of the family,' looking up at him in her bright way. 'Now, don't scowl at me about it, because that frightens me and doesn't become you. You know I would go willingly if I could.'

'Can't Mr. Erle put off his walk?'

'I wouldn't ask him to do so; he is not up to it every day, but this afternoon he feels fit for anything, he says.'

'Then you won't come?'

'You see I can't, Claude,' deprecatingly.

He turned away with an oath.

'Claude!' she exclaimed, her face flushing indignantly.

'I beg your pardon, Laura; but it is such nonsense! Come along, and let Teddy go with your father. It isn't too far for him.'

'I never throw papa over for any one,' she said firmly. 'I am much obliged for your kind thought of me, but I cannot go.'

'Very well; that settles it,' angrily; and lifting his hat he strode away, leaving her with that painful sense and dread of his 'touchiness' which always came over her when he gave way to one of his 'tantrums,' as he did frequently enough. Life with him was a precarious pleasure to a woman. Before men he exercised some degree of self-restraint; but not the changing sea, the varying wind, or any unsettled thing one can think of in nature, was more unstable than his temper in dealing with women. The very slightest expression of dissent from his wishes or opinions was fatal to his serenity, and it took him hours to recover his equanimity. He went back to Enleigh now, his face as black as a thunder-cloud, and told Mrs. Elliott shortly that he would not go to Oaklands.

'Can't Laura come?' asked Audrey.

'No; she chooses instead to go tearing over the hills with her father; tiring herself to death to see some confounded old woman.'

Mrs. Elliott did her best to make him change his resolution, and being unable to do so started for the drive in anything but a seraphic frame of mind herself.

Audrey had to bear the brunt of the storm. The lady was critical at all times; when she was at all put out she became hypercritical. There was not a feature in her niece's face, a point in her appearance or manner, an article of her dress, which she did not pass under review.

'That ride to Glynton in the sun has ruined your complexion, Audrey, and as that was the only good thing about you, you are not fit to be seen now. Your eyes are nondescript, or green, if they are anything, and your nose frightful. I wonder you don't wear a hat that would hide it a little.'

'I don't know what sort of hat would hide my nose, aunt Eleanor,' said poor Audrey meekly, as if apologising for the existence of her vituperated organ, which, however, was by no means of so despicable a kind as her relation's remark implied. It was a very characteristic little nose, at all events; and though, perhaps, not so provokingly designed by Providence for men to hang their hearts upon as her friend Laura's, was yet impertinent and expressive enough to be a charming feature in her face.

'A hat with a brim would hide your deformities in some degree,' went on Mrs. Elliott. 'That one you have on is like a milk-bowl turned upside down. I suppose you think it looks well to have it come down just to show your eyebrows. You won't have any left soon, that is one consolation. Your veil will speedily rub them all off, besides destroying the little bit of complexion you have left.'

'I put a veil on to keep the flies from tormenting me; it is very thin,' in an exculpatory voice.

A pause, during which Mrs. Elliott scanned her victim from head to foot, and the victim, for the thousandth time, was enabled to picture what vivisection must be like.

'Is that the latest fashion in neckties? Adopted from your maid, I suppose? She rules you. It looks like a wisp.'

'It is a sailor's knot, and Claude thought it very pretty.' Audrey always tried to shield herself by quoting some authority it was possible her persecutor might respect.

'Indeed! then we shall have Laura bursting out all over with sailors' knots.'

'It's very hot,' remarked Audrey cheerfully, hoping to divert attention from herself.

'It is hot. I don't wonder you feel it, however; the tight gloves you wear must stop the circulation. I wonder you can bear them.

'They are not tighter than gloves ought to be,' said Audrey, almost in despair at this fresh attack, as she looked at her small delicately-gloved hands.

'Aren't they? People with large hands always wear tight gloves; I have observed that before.'

'I always have six and three-quarters. If I had sevens, they would be like boats on me; besides they wear out so.'

'I'm glad you think of economy sometimes. You will have to marry a millionaire to enable you to go on spending and dressing at the rate you do now, or rather to enable your maid to do so.'

Miss Dashwood's maid was a sore subject. She liked her, which fact was enough to insure her aunt's dislike.

'As your own fortune will soon be quite insufficient for your wants, I advise you to turn your attention to this millionaire chandler who is come to the Abbey. He could, at all events, pay your bills, and as he wants family, like all parvenus, he would probably take you.'

'Probably, aunt Eleanor, when I signify my wishes to him. I will take some lessons from the Miss Ellises; they have had a good deal of experience in that line. My only fear is that they may anticipate me. As Mrs. Ellis did not wait for you to call on her before coming to Enleigh, I should not wonder if young Mr. de Montmorency found a carriage waiting for him at the Hillingdon station to take him at once to Oaklands on his arrival. Possession is nine points of the law, isn't it?'

When Mrs. Elliott had goaded her victims into a retort, she generally subsided herself for a little while, and on this occasion they had got near Oaklands before she resumed her criticisms.

At that same moment Audrey and her nose were the subject of conversation at the very place to which they were going. There three young ladies were reposing in easy-chairs, under the shade of a magnificent ash-tree. The lawn was as smooth as a billiard-table, and there was a grand display of croquet balls and mallets.

The heads of the three young ladies were thrown back, as if in contemplation of the rustling ash-leaves above, with the blue sky gleaming through them. They may have looked at the sky; it is possible; but they were chiefly engaged in watching in divine enjoyment the smoke curling up from three cigarettes which they held between their respective lips.

'How delicious this is!' exclaimed Violet, flinging away the end of hers. 'Give me another, Georgie. How I hope no one will call! Entertaining the natives is such a bore!'

'There is no one to call, except the Dashwoods; and I doubt Miss Audrey's giving herself the trouble to do that.'

'I hate that girl!' remarked Violet, as she lit a fresh cigarette; ' she is the most odious, stuck-up,'—not being able to fix on a substantive sufficiently indicative of her dislike, she ended with an expressive ' Oh!'

Miss Violet looked the very personification of soulless enjoyment as she thus delivered herself. She was exceedingly pretty. No one could see her without being sensible of her sweet youthful charm. There was neither mind nor soul in her face, but in the mere externals of beauty, in form and colouring, in almost childlike grace and playfulness, it would not have been easy to find her equal. Her eyes were dancing, sunny blue; her hair golden brown, and literally 'running over' with rippling curls, which even the appalling head-gear she had on could not conceal; her blooming wild-rose complexion, her pretty fairy figure, and perfect hands and feet, all combined to make her as fair a picture—though not of a lofty type—as it was possible to conceive. But the loveliness was mortal, and nothing more. It would never suggest grand thoughts of a noble life to be nobly lived; and Violet certainly did not look noble when she went on to remark:

'I do hope Miss Audrey won't take it into her head to call! Just pick up some of those cigarette-ends, Kate. The whole place is strewed.'

'What fun it would be if she did!' exclaimed Georgie. 'I wonder what she would say!'

'Nothing to us; she would curl her lip and turn up her odious little nose in disdainful silence, and then go away and abuse us behind our backs.'

Now, as a rule, none of the Miss Ellises made any secret of their devotion to cigarettes and other narcotic delights—a devotion maintained by them to be perfectly innocent in itself, as indeed it was; but in the present instance there was a very potent reason for departure from their ordinary candour on the subject.

Audrey Dashwood they hated, and no keener gratification could they have had than that of shocking her, had she alone been concerned; but she was the sister of 'a fish'—by that name did Violet frankly designate every man with the least pretensions to 'eligibility' —and though Claude was not a fish of the first or even the second quality, yet he was not to be despised in case no more desirable creature 'bit.'

Of course every one would like to catch a salmon, but when salmon are not to be had, a salmon-trout, a perch, or even a pike, is not to be contemned. It is true Claude was a second son, but he had no younger brothers, and his mother's fortune was settled on him; he was a barrister, too, with a reputation already sufficiently risen to be an earnest of further elevation; he was, besides, a *littérateur* of some note. Violet certainly meant to 'go in' for a salmon, but it was possible she might be forced to a reversionary interest in Claude, and she was too skilful a sportswoman not to know the sort of fly with which to bait her hook.

To do her justice, she had no immediate design on Claude. He was the last sort of man she would have wished to marry, but being resolved not to follow her sisters' example, she, while throwing for a salmon, would not reject a trout. Accordingly she would not be seen by him, or any one belonging to him, in the act of smoking rather potent cigarettes. That was a bait to which she felt instinctively he would never rise. Her dismay therefore, the dismay of the whole party, may be conceived, when, as they were picturing to themselves the felicity which might result from horrifying Audrey, they suddenly became aware of the approach of a carriage.

'Good heavens, there's some one coming to call!' cried Kate.

'*Parler du diable!*' exclaimed Violet; 'it's the Dashwoods. Pick up those cigarette-ends, Georgie, do! Is there time to escape? what shall we do?'

'No, they would see us; it is too late. Don't all jump up in that way,' remonstrated Kate.

Violet had sprung up, and was hastily collecting the white paper remnants of the exhausted cigarettes. 'How abominably we shall smell! We don't know her well enough to kiss her, that's one blessing!' she ejaculated pantingly between her labours.

'It's not the Dashwoods,' said Georgie; 'you needn't fuss.'

'Yes, it is. I know the horses, and it's the Dashwood livery. Georgie, what a fool you are to go on laughing like that! Hide the cigar-box under the lilac-tree, will you?'

Georgie Ellis's sense of fun was so great, that even at the risk of losing a desirable fish she had to yield to it, and she was now choking with laughter. 'If only St. Clare was here, we might put it on him,' she remarked, pushing the box under the shrub.

'How vilely we do smell, though!' exclaimed Violet in despair, as Mrs. Elliott and

Audrey, perceiving the young ladies on the lawn, came forward.

As they drew near, the three girls vigorously inhaled draughts of fresh air, hoping thereby to dispel the fumes they had reason to fear still hung about them.

'That odious Audrey is sure to smell out something with that hateful little sharp nose of hers!' whispered Violet viciously, as Miss Dashwood, whose unfortunate olfactory organ was thus a second time made the subject of animadversion, approached.

In the confusion and alarm of the first moment Violet had thrown her cigarette on the chair from which in her amazed haste she had arisen. As the visitors came up she caught sight of it, still in a state of combustion.

There was but one resource. Extinction was impossible under the circumstances: she therefore dexterously contrived to slip it into her pocket, burning her fingers much in the process, and at the imminent risk of setting fire to her dainty handkerchief and the letter, written on flimsy foreign paper, which she had that morning received from her friend, Colonel Wilmot.

As they were sitting down she espied a cigarette, which must have fallen out of the box, close to Audrey's chair. Kate's glances directed towards the same spot convinced her that she was not alone in her discovery. The situation was critical. The burning cigarette in her pocket exercised her terribly. It might at any moment cause an awkward sensation by setting fire to her dress, and it would in any case burn a hole in Colonel Wilmot's letter. She gradually insinuated her hand into the receptacle in question to feel how matters were progressing there.

Unfortunately her fingers came in contact with the ignited end, and it needed all her self-command to suppress an exclamation and start. She did suppress them, however, and succeeded in extinguishing the enemy, though at considerable injury to the letter and her own pretty little fingers.

Mrs. Ellis, who soon appeared, received

Mrs. Elliott with all the consideration due by the mother of six disposable daughters to a clever woman known to have influence over disposable young men. With respect to the latter Oaklands was fortunately situated. The neighbourhood abounded in good preserves.

There was Glynton absolutely asking for a mistress; so dull and lonely that its lord, young, good-looking, and above all rich, was fain, in order to escape its gloom, to accept the hospitality of strangers. There was Enleigh, with Claude—only a silver fish, it is true; but also with his friend, Mr. Carew, young, rich, and though said to be somewhat eccentric, yet reputed to be 'good' even to religiousness, and that, though by no means a *sine quâ non*, does count for something. It is a pleasant adjunct to a man's other qualifications, and adds to his market value, especially in the eyes of dowagers of the better sort.

Mrs. Ellis felt herself honoured by the presence of this 'good' young man's mother in her house. It might lead to his own. She regretted that Lady Emily Carew was out a this moment. The latter would have been so glad to see Mrs. Elliott, and hear directly from her how her son was. Unfortunately she was gone for a walk with Margaret.

'Why, there they are!' cried Violet. 'What on earth has happened, Meg?'

As she spoke, a lady, rather but not very stout, accompanied by a girl whose dress was in the utmost disorder, came through a gate leading on to the lawn.

'Ah, my dears, my dears,' began the former in a voice so excited that she could hardly articulate, 'we've been all but dead! Thank God you see us alive! that we are not all dead corpses, with nothing left of us but our clothes! Ah, my dearest, best of friends,' addressing Mrs. Ellis, 'how right you were to advise me not to go so far!'

Every one naturally asked for an explanation, whence it appeared that the two ladies had met a herd of cattle which had caused them great alarm.

'Do sit down, Lady Emily, you must be tired,' said Mrs. Ellis.

'Tired! Well, no. I'm too much frightened and surprised to think such creatures should be allowed to range the country at will. We should both be at this moment corpses, my dear friend,' impressively, 'had it not been for *the* most beautiful and charming young lady I ever met, and her father.'

'It must have been Laura and Mr. Erle,' said Audrey.

'Ah, my dear Audrey!' turning to her; 'I beg your pardon; and Mrs. Elliott! Dear Mrs. Elliott, excuse my rudeness in not having spoken to you,' rising and kissing both with effusion. 'I saw you, but I was so frightened. Laura, yes; that was the young lady's name,' eagerly to Audrey; 'such a dear girl; so courteous and well-bred! No fineladyish airs and graces about her; and she did not laugh at our fright or think us fools, did she, Margaret?'

Audrey bethought herself that if Miss Laura did not do so before Lady Emily, she probably indemnified herself afterwards for the self-control.

'But what was it? I don't understand,' said Mrs. Ellis.

'Well, now, I'll tell you all in order, exactly as it happened;' and Lady Emily sat down, settling herself regularly for a story in due form.

Her stories were terrible. She lost herself in them, and her hearers lost their patience. Wishing to be graphic, she succeeded only in missing any point there may have been in her narrative.

'As you know, my dears, Margaret and I started for a walk. I must just explain,' turning to Mrs. Elliott and Audrey, 'that I like to take a walk every day, for I'm a little inclined to be stout, unfortunately; and my dear son Harold has such a horror of very stout people; not that I'm very stout, because I take so much exercise. Do you think I'm stouter than when you saw me last, my dear?' to Audrey.

'By no means, Lady Emily. I find you much thinner,' replied Miss Dashwood, with great tact.

'I'm glad of that. Indeed, I hardly know how I could get stout, I eat so little and I walk so much. I've quite given up cream, and I take such a tiny, tiny bit of sugar in my tea, don't I, dear Mrs. Ellis? though I can't bear tea without sugar; but it is all to please my dear son Harold,' with a half-shy laugh, as if apologising for her affection; 'you see, he is my only child, the only one I ever had,' regretfully, 'and I naturally like to do what he wishes.'

'But he wouldn't wish you to starve yourself, surely, Lady Emily?'

'My dear, no!' in utter repudiation of such an idea. 'On the contrary, he always scolds me for not taking cream, and comes and puts it into my cup himself when he is at home; so touching of him, dear boy!' tenderly; 'and I just take it to satisfy him when he is there,' with a confidential nod, 'and then when he is away I never touch it.'

They had got a long way from the herd of cattle, and the young ladies were almost convulsed with laughter.

'But about the cows, Lady Emily?' said Violet, recalling her to the point.

'I'm coming to them, my dear. I had just to explain about the walking. Well, as I said, Margaret and I started for our walk— so kind of dear Margaret to come with me; I go with my maid when I can't get any one else; though, indeed, I sometimes fancy she doesn't like taking such long walks; and I am always glad when I can get any one else to come, and Margaret is so kind about it; indeed, so is Violet, so are you all, my dears,' with comprehensive gratitude. 'Well — where was I? O yes; I remember. We started, Margaret and I, and were going very calmly and quietly along such a pretty lane, but so narrow, only just room enough for us two, and we were admiring this beautiful country and talking about all sorts of things. We had got on to really quite clever subjects, hadn't we, dear Margaret? all about history, you know, and all that, and about how ignorant people are in general; it was quite interesting, and I was just wishing that my dear

Harold had been there to hear us'—Audrey's knowledge of the gentleman led her to think it fortunate that he was not—' when, O my dears, the most awful sight burst upon our view. The whole lane was alive with bulls!' and she paused, that her listeners might fully take in the gravity of the situation. ' Bulls, my dear friends; I never saw so many together before! I hardly thought the world contained so many bulls.'

But Lady Emily's story, told in her own words, would fill at least twenty pages. The sense of her inordinate amount of verbiage was that she and her companion had been much alarmed at the so-called 'bulls,' and in order to escape them had clambered over a gate into a field which, to their inexpressible horror, they found to be also full of oxen. Animated by the curiosity natural to them, these harmless and gentle creatures had advanced to inspect the strangers who had entered their domain in such unseemly haste. In an access of terror, Lady Emily adjured her friend to save herself by jumping into the ditch, and then abandoned herself to her own fate, when a merciful Providence sent to her aid two angels in the shape of a young lady and an old gentleman, who drove off the oxen, helped Miss Ellis out of the ditch, and revived their drooping courage by administering some wine which the lady happened to be carrying to a sick person.

'But, indeed, it was a terrible moment,' concluded Lady Emily, 'when I found myself alone amongst those raging creatures! I thought of the Christians thrown to the lions and tigers; at least I'm not sure now if they ever were thrown; I rather think my son says they were not; in fact, I get a little confused between the things that did happen and those that didn't. And you know this young lady, my dear Audrey?' she continued. 'Tell me all about her. I must go and call upon her. If I only had had a daughter like that! I have always so longed for a daughter!'

When the visitors had taken their departure, and Lady Emily had gone in to repose after her adventures, Violet related to her sister the story of Mrs. Elliott's inopportune arrival, congratulating herself much on the heroism she had displayed. 'It was quite noble!' she exclaimed, pulling the cigarette from her pocket, and holding up her fingers to exhibit the damage they had sustained in extinguishing it. 'I am sure I once read about a man who poked his hand into the fire for some great object—only I forget what the object was—and held it there for ever so long; but he was nothing to me! I'll keep that cigarette as a trophy; but I must have another now;' and she proceeded to light it, looking inexpressibly comic as she settled her small graceful person in a capacious chair, and began puffing away—under difficulties, however, —for her pretty lips would curve with an irresistible impulse towards laughter when she recalled the 'stampede' Audrey's arrival had occasioned.

CHAPTER VII.

Lady Emily Carew lost no time in calling at the Rectory. She was both profuse and diffuse in her thanks, astonishing the undemonstrative Mrs. Erle by embracing her warmly, and gratifying her by the praises she bestowed on Laura.

'You have so many daughters,' she said in a tone of envious regret, 'and I, who have always longed for one, have none. How happy I should be if I had a dear, charming, affectionate girl like yours! And so pretty too! And I like pretty people.'

'I wish I could steal you, my dear,' holding Laura's hand lingeringly as she was going away, and lavishing on her sundry caresses, much to the amazement of that lively damsel, who had amused Audrey and her own family not a little by her version of the encounter with the 'bulls;' which turned out to be a herd of very harmless Welsh cattle, guiltless of any goring or tossing intentions.

'We first heard the most dreadful screams,' said Laura; 'and when we saw Lady Emily, she was standing, her hands clasped and her eyes shut, praying aloud, not to be saved from the "bulls," which she evidently thought useless, but to be forgiven all her past offences, and petitioning Heaven with all her might to bless and protect her darling and much-loved Harold. It really was quite tragic, only when I pictured to myself her much-loved son's sarcastic face, and the scorn with which he would have treated her fears, I could hardly help laughing.'

'But you didn't laugh; that was what delighted her.'

'No; it would have been inhuman just then. She was absolutely blanched with terror; and it was real heroism, for I firmly believe she thought her last hour was come; yet her one idea was to keep the bulls—as she persisted in calling the poor animals—from discovering Miss Ellis's hiding-place.'

Lady Emily, in relating her adventure, had said nothing of those screams which had attracted Mr. Erle and Laura. It was her one bit of disingenuousness. Her propensity to give utterance to a prolonged series of shrieks when alarmed was one which her dear son never failed to reprehend in his most caustic manner. In indulging in it on the present occasion, she felt she had transgressed his wishes; but she would confess the delinquency to himself alone, trusting that he would forgive her in consideration of the sufferings she had undergone.

Lady Emily's sudden fancy for Laura was a great consolation to Mrs. Elliott. She hoped it would be the means of removing that dangerously attractive damsel for some time out of the way of her infatuated nephew; for Lady Emily had invited her to Melbury, and though nothing definite had been settled, Mrs. Elliott resolved that the scheme should not fall through for want of a little judicious management on her part.

In spite of Claude's very decided opposition, she asked Lady Emily to come to Enleigh after her visit to Oaklands. She would thus have an opportunity of seeing more of Laura, and her coming might induce Harold to prolong his stay, and thus have the impression deepened which Mrs. Elliott felt very sure her lively neighbour had made on him. His moody sarcasms, whenever the latter was mentioned, had not escaped her keen observation. She noticed how intently his eyes followed every movement of the graceful girlish figure. The look in his eyes was not, it is true, one of admiration; it was rather one of repulsion; but the lady knew that hate and love are but varying forms of the same feeling, and that when the hate is felt by a young man, and the object of it is a beautiful young woman, it is very likely to transform itself into love.

All men are, of course, wolves, whom it behoves all women to avoid—if they can; but Laura, being highly impecunious, must consent to accept a husband, and Mrs. Elliott's earnest desire was that that husband should not be Claude. She did not wish to have her, poor, and loving devotedly every member of her equally poor family, for a niece-in-law. She would always be wanting Claude to do something for her needy brothers, and trying to get her pretty sisters on in the world.

But if Harold Carew liked to undertake the office of benefactor to the Erle family, well and good. Mrs. Elliott would feel sincere pleasure in her sparkling neighbour's prosperity; and Harold was so eccentric and cared so little for what the world said, that she thought it not unlikely he might take it into his head to marry his mother's new friend.

Claude had resented Laura's refusal to go to Oaklands so highly that he sulked for more than a week; nor did Lady Emily's visit to the Rectory add to the sweetness of his temper. He would have repudiated with scorn the idea that he feared Harold as a rival, or entertained any jealousy of him. Nevertheless he, too, had observed the sarcasms and gloomy looks which had attracted Mrs. Elliott's attention, and showed himself much averse to any intimacy between the houses of Carew and Erle. He did not apprehend that Harold would, of his own accord, wish to possess himself of his treasure, but the treasure might, at any moment, take it into her head to 'convert' that eccentric scholar, and if she once undertook the task, 'it would be all up with Carew;' that was Mr. Dashwood's conclusion; he felt the young lady's influence to be so potent over himself that he could not conceive its being less so over other men.

CHAPTER VIII.

'John is come!'

This was the exclamation that greeted Laura one afternoon as she entered the rectory garden on her return from the village.

John was her brother, who had lately left Oxford, and was now waiting on Providence and his friends to find him employment.

Laura was devoted to him, and rushed joyfully to meet him. She saw at once that something was wrong, but to her eager inquiries he answered that all was well. When they were alone, however, he threw off the mask.

'Laura, I'm in a deuce of a fix, and if you can't help me out of it, I'm hanged if I know what to do.'

This was nothing new. As long as she could remember, her brother had been getting into fixes, and leaving her to get him out of them.

'What is it, dear?' she asked now.

'I may as well make a clean breast of it, though you will blame me, of course—you always do; but if I can get clear of this, I'll keep straight—I will, upon my honour! And, Laura, it is hardly my fault. I couldn't live at Oxford on the miserable pittance the governor allowed me.'

'How much is it?' she asked, her heart suddenly feeling like lead.

'Well, a hundred, or a hundred and fifty would keep things quiet just till I get something to do.'

A hundred! a hundred and fifty! What a paltry sum! Quite ludicrous to those who count their debts by thousands; but on Laura's ear the numbers fell almost like a death-sentence. Where or how could she procure a hundred pounds? The slender resources of the family were strained to the utmost as it was. It was impossible that they could meet this additional demand.

'A hundred and fifty!' she exclaimed; 'O John, how is papa to get a hundred and fifty pounds? Who is the man? Is it a pressing debt?' she went on, feeling that remonstrance was useless, and anxious to know the worst.

By degrees it came out that he had been considerably involved before leaving Oxford, but had said nothing about it, hoping, when he got something to do, to be able to clear off the most pressing claims. He had been intended for the Church; but he had so frequently urged, and so completely proved, his unfitness for it, that Mr. Erle, with many regrets over the money expended on his University career, had reluctantly consented to his abandoning all idea of a clerical calling. He was now a gentleman at large. His expectations from his friends were large too, and he was always fruitful in suggestions to them as to the means to be employed for procuring his advancement. He had a suggestion for Laura now.

He was eager to prevent his father from learning anything of his difficulties, and in order to do so, proposed that his sister should borrow the money from Audrey Dashwood, or rather, through her, from Claude.

'John!' she exclaimed, 'I would just as soon kill myself as ask Audrey or Claude for money. What can you be thinking of?'

His face fell.

'I don't see why you shouldn't. What is the use of having rich friends if you don't make use of them? Claude—'

'John, nothing on earth would induce me to ask Claude Dashwood for money,' colouring to the roots of her hair.

'Then what am I to do?' he asked in despair. 'I counted on you to help me. It is deuced hard on me to have to live like a gentleman and mix with other fellows on nothing.'

'No harder than it is on me. How absurd it would be for me to attempt to dress like Audrey! But all that is beside the point. The thing is, what is to be done now? Borrowing from the Dashwoods is out of the question. I would rather die than apply to hem.'

'Then I don't see how I am to keep it

from the governor,' he began, fixing on the consideration he knew would move her most.

'We must do that at all hazards. The very thought of your owing such a sum would kill him. As it is, mamma is breaking her heart about him. He grows more feeble every day, yet he talks of giving up his one holiday in the year because of the expense, and now— O John!' in an accent of despairing surprise, as she felt to what sacrifices her own devotion to her father could have nerved her, 'how was it that your love for him didn't teach you self-denial, knowing as you do how sensitive he is on the subject of debt?'

She was young, or she would not have asked the question. Affection does not teach the John Erles of this world self-denial. He looked weakly ashamed of himself, yet answered half-impatiently,

'Laura, it's no good pitching into a fellow, or crying over spilt milk.'

'It is great good for you to feel that you have been as weak as water,' she answered quickly. 'What you have done would half kill papa if he knew it. Will the man wait? Can you put him off a little?'

'I've done that so often, you see, hoping to get something—'

'That he will wait no longer. I see. Who is the man? If I wrote and guaranteed the money, or some of it, in six months, would he wait?'

He had told her that he would make a clean breast of it, but he had not done so, nor was he by any means disposed to do so. He shuffled now and parried her questions, so that she could not arrive at anything definite. The truth was, his debts amounted to nearer three hundred than a hundred and fifty, and though the former, like the latter, sum may appear ludicrously small to some people, it was not so to him. He shrank from telling his sister the real state of his affairs, helpless as he felt.

He had been mean enough, or foolish enough, to get into debt; but he was not, it will be seen, reckless enough to have recourse to those philanthropic benefactors of mankind who so persistently offer to relieve gentlemen from their difficulties—for a consideration.

This heroism may possibly have resulted from the fact that Mr. Erle had no expectations, nothing to make it worth any one's while to be benevolent to him; so that his applications might have met with less attention from those philanthropists than the expansive nature of their announcements would lead simple people to suppose.

John scouted the idea of Laura's writing to 'the man.' Such a proceeding was, he averred, out of the question. What value would any tradesman attach to her word? Besides, how could she guarantee the money?

'Simply enough. I would earn it.'

Earn it! Had she proposed starting for the moon, he could not have looked more surprised.

'Yes, earn it. I shall get an engagement as a governess. I could teach strangers as well as my own brothers and sisters, and Amy is old enough to manage the children and help mamma now.'

'Talk of killing papa! That would do it and no mistake,' said John, relapsing in his surprise into the old childish way of speaking of his father.

'Not at all; he would feel the parting, of course; so should I,' with a sort of sob in her voice; 'but there would be no disgrace; and if I got eighty or a hundred pounds a year, in three years your debts would be paid, for I could easily dress on twenty pounds a year. I dress on far less now. Besides, you would get something in the mean time.'

'But you would have to tell papa and mamma your reason for going.'

'No; I have been thinking of trying to be a governess for some time. There is no reason why I should not be one. Papa ought to have a curate,'—John winced; had he fulfilled the paternal wish, he might now have been of some use,—'and if I could do something, he might manage it. These bills of yours will take all the money at first, of course, but afterwards—'

'Laura, I will repay you the money the instant I can.'

He was always strong in promises. They cost nothing, and soothed his conscience for the moment. Besides, we none of us like to have it tacitly assumed that we are absolutely good for nothing.

'There is another thing, John,' went on the girl, not, it is to be feared, much impressed by the prospect of her brother's performances; 'I have written a story—and I thought, perhaps—I did not know—one hears of people getting so much money nowadays; and if I could get some in that way, the bills could be paid off at once.'

John Erle had immense faith in his sister's infinite resource and capacity for getting him out of scrapes, but none at all in her literary ability. Woman as a money-earning animal, except under the familiar form of a governess, was a new and irreceivable idea to him.

'Yes, one hears of it,' he said doubtfully, 'but I didn't know that you were clever enough for that sort of thing.'

'If I could only get some money in that way we might clear off your debts very soon, much sooner, at all events, than by waiting till I can earn the money as a governess,' went on Laura, continuing to assume, unconsciously almost, that the task of paying his debts would be devolved by her brother on some other than himself. That that other should not be her father was her great object.

'If you could get money, it would be an awfully good thing,' remarked Mr. Erle; 'but I don't know how I can help you,' and he proposed instead that she should consult Audrey Dashwood. He was willing that every one should assist her except himself. This unwillingness to act proceeded from no want of affection. It was grounded, partly on a secret distrust of himself, partly on a sort of fear he entertained of the novel line she was adopting.

He could not have defined the feeling, but he was possessed with the idea that the course she proposed was, in some way, unusual, and, perhaps, not *the thing*.

'I wish you would consult Audrey,' he repeated. 'You know Claude writes, and he would be able to advise you.'

'I don't want to tell Claude anything about it,' she said, colouring vividly, as she always did at his name; 'and I would rather not tell Audrey. I am sure you could manage it if you would try. If it fails, no harm has been done.'

'It makes a fellow feel like a fool if a thing fails,' he remarked, somewhat ruefully.

'I feel much more like a fool sitting down supinely and doing nothing, while papa gets more broken every day, and dear mamma looks so worn and anxious. What does it signify whether one looks like a fool or not?'

He continued, however, to urge his unfitness for the task, going back to his original idea that she should borrow the money. That seemed to him a far more direct way of procuring it. Earning it was slow work. As she still declined, he said, 'I say, Laura, you must give up the thought of being a governess.

It would never do. Why, all your friends would cut you.'

'They wouldn't be worth keeping then. Audrey wouldn't, or the Dashwoods;' but there were doubt and a questioning sound in her voice as she looked at him.

'Claude wouldn't like it,' he said significantly.

'And what is Claude to me?' she retorted quickly, almost angrily. 'I certainly shall not regulate my actions to suit his fancies.'

Nevertheless Claude was very much to her. He was at the root of her resolution to try her fortune as a governess. She felt every day more and more how he interfered with her peace of mind. Watching for his coming and going, thinking of what he had said at their last meeting and what he would say at their next, came between her and all her usual occupations. Her task of teaching was an utter weariness to her. She was remorsefully conscious of irritability towards the young brothers and sisters, who had always been accustomed to turn to her for help and sympathy. Their spirits, the stories of their little joys and sorrows, fretted and tried her as they had never done before.

She felt impelled, by an infinite longing, to be alone with her great happiness, her pleasant misery, her bright memories; but being wholly unselfish, sensible, and practical, as well as sensitively conscientious, in spite of her apparent volatility, she knew that such isolation would be the basest desertion of her duty. She was, besides, too high-spirited to be a mere waiter on Claude's good pleasure. 'If he liked me well enough to want me to be his wife, he might have asked me by this time,' she argued; 'if he does not, and is only amusing himself at my expense, I decline to be made the plaything of an idle hour, and then flung aside.' So she wisely resolved not to let him wreck her life, but rather to leave her home, and see if, haply, time and change would break the spell. She could not afford the luxury of cherishing a romantic *grande passion;* yet the thought of what Claude would say was never absent from her mind.

She lay awake all that night in feverish anxiety and excitement.

She was so constituted that everything she felt was a passion. She enjoyed rapturously and suffered acutely. Her love for her parents, for her brothers and sisters, for Audrey, was passionate in its depth. Her love for Claude was deep and tender too, but it was tempered by the consciousness that it was unsolicited, in words at least, and by some latent distrust of him which she shrank from analysing.

Knowing she could not leave her home to become a governess without Audrey's knowledge, she resolved to consult her on the subject, and ask her help in obtaining some employment.

Audrey was both surprised and distressed when the scheme was unfolded to her, though she could not but approve of it under the circumstances as described by Laura, who, however, said nothing of her brother's debts.

'John said you would repudiate me if I became a governess,' she said, a dewy look in her dark eyes.

'I'm sorry John takes me for such a snob. I think it quite splendid of you,' throwing her arms round her. 'In your place I should do exactly the same; but O, Laura, how I shall miss you!'

CHAPTER IX.

The announcement of Laura's intention caused a sort of moral earthquake at Enleigh. It affected several people there materially. It would make or mar Mrs. Elliott's plans, by either forcing Claude to propose at once or effectually preventing his ever doing so.

Lady Emily Carew heard the proposal with regret too. It would interfere with her scheme of having Laura to visit her at Melbury, to which she had been looking forward with great delight. Such a visit would entirely relieve the tedium of the coming winter. Now she could not hope for it, but, though disappointed herself, her admiration and sympathy were increased tenfold for the girl who was willing to make such an effort.

'It will be a sad life for a gay, bright little thing like her to be a governess!' she exclaimed that evening in the drawing-room. 'Even if the people she goes to are nice, she will miss the love and devotion she has always been used to. In fact, I can hardly imagine her a governess at all. She is so—so—I don't know what—so bright somehow; don't you agree with me, dear Harold?'

That was the usual finale to all Lady Emily's remarks if her dear son happened to be present. The circumstance that he very rarely did agree with her did not lessen the frequency of the appeal. On this occasion, however, she was fortunate enough to have made an observation in which he could concur. He confessed dryly that he could not imagine Miss Erle a governess, adding, in a somewhat disparaging tone, that if her pupils were to become proficients in anything but flippancy, she must learn to control her tongue a little.

Lady Emily, always happily unconscious of his sarcasms, went on innocently:

'Yes, indeed; it must be so trying always to have to be setting a good example! I remember my dear old French governess used to make me write dictation from Noël et Chapsal's Exercises, because *les sentiments étaient si beaux*, she said; and I suppose she hoped they would do me good.'

'Poor Laura!' said Digby. 'Fancy her tied down to instilling *les beaux sentiments* into a lot of stupid girls! How bored she will be!'

'Why doesn't she marry?' asked Harold.

Here Mrs. Elliott felt that the situation was becoming critical, and that it would be wise to interpose. Claude had not spoken, but she knew instinctively that he was looking very black behind his newspaper. Of what was he thinking?

'It is not every man who would care to marry the eldest of such a large and needy family,' she remarked. 'It is a great responsibility, especially as she is so wrapped up in them. You see, she doesn't hesitate at anything where they are concerned.'

'Poor girl!' said Lady Emily, a world of sympathy in her voice. 'Aren't you sorry for her, dear Harold?'

Dear Harold could not conscientiously say he felt at all sorry for Miss Erle. Sorrow was not the emotion she awoke in him.

'I should say she could take very good care of herself, mother,' he returned; 'but I doubt her success as a governess. Why doesn't she write instead? I should think she was better suited for it than for teaching. The flippant style of writing that is the fashion now would just suit her. I have little doubt she could turn out any number of articles full of the silly chaff on serious subjects which goes down in these days.'

Miss Dashwood resented highly this depreciation of her friend.

'I should think any children exceedingly fortunate who had Laura for a governess,' she exclaimed warmly. 'She is the best and noblest girl I ever knew; never thinking about herself at all. I should have said that the efforts of a girl struggling to help those she loves were deserving of something better than sneers; but I observe that generous sympathy is as much out of fashion now as courtesy.'

Lady Emily looked puzzled and slightly alarmed. Being herself so accustomed to her son's peculiarities of speech and manner as rarely to be disturbed by them, she could not understand the discomposing effect they had on strangers. She looked at Audrey deprecatingly, while Harold's own face assumed the expression it invariably did whenever the fact was forced on him that Nature, while denying to women, for purposes of her own, great physical strength, has yet very effectually compensated for the deficiency by endowing them with eyes and—tongues. No man ever made him feel 'small' as did these creatures miscalled weak. The snubbed look on his countenance struggled now, too, with some real regret. He was very kind-hearted, and when once convinced he had given pain was always compunctious. Besides, he liked Audrey. He was sure she did not want to marry him, and could therefore comfortably gratify in her society the curiosity those impulsive, loquacious fascinations aroused in him; a curiosity which dread of their 'designs' generally kept him from satisfying.

'I beg your pardon,' he said, in as exculpatory a tone as the asperity of his nature permitted him to adopt; 'I had no intention whatever of sneering at your friend, and the suggestion I made was kindly meant, at least.'

'Yes, indeed,' interrupted Lady Emily, desirous of justifying her offspring in the eyes of the company; 'and I'm sure, Audrey, you are mistaken in saying he meant to sneer. Sneering is such a horrible thing. Isn't there some play or story that has a dreadful man or woman called Sneer or Sneerwell in it? all so odious and ill-natured. I'm sure my dear son would never be so ungenerous as to sneer at that charming girl's wish to help her parents,' in a tone of gentle dignity, all her maternal feathers beautifully ruffled.

'Well, we won't discuss Laura's private affairs any more,' returned Audrey, still experiencing a glow of anger, but speaking gently to Lady Emily, as she always did.

It was well she had come to such a conclusion. Claude had borne as much as he could well bear. He put down his paper with ominous silence, and rose, his face very white.

'It would have been wiser not to have discussed them at all,' he said, in a low but perfectly distinct voice of smothered wrath. 'I can only be surprised that you permitted such a discussion, Audrey, or joined in it;' and he left the room.

He was in a paroxysm of anger with his sister, with the Carews, with his aunt, with Laura herself. He felt personally insulted at hearing her name bandied about, and her money-earning capabilities talked over in this way. How had Harold Carew ventured to speak thus slightingly of her—above all, to propose her writing!

Claude hated a literary woman, with an intense unreasoning hatred. If Laura ever took such an idea into her head, he told himself now, with much mental strong language, he would have done with her for ever.

And how had she dared to lay herself

open to these remarks, by proposing such an extraordinary scheme as leaving her home to become a governess!

In his secret heart his idea was that she should have waited patiently till it suited his good will and pleasure to come to some decision respecting her.

He had not quite made up his mind about marrying her. Unconsciously, and consciously too, he was influenced by Mrs. Elliott's arguments, but he could not resolve to give Laura up. Whenever he tried to do so, the thousand threads by which she had wound herself round his heart gave such potent proof of their existence, that life became a torture.

Still he had not wanted to decide hastily. There was plenty of time, and he was well satisfied with things as they were.

Laura's thus taking the initiative altered everything. It forced him to come to some decision. Under his own eye at Smedston she was safe; it would be otherwise if she went out into the world to rough it among strangers—a governess. The thought drove him into a frenzy. He swore aloud with anger against her for conceiving such a plan, or, worse still, for speaking of it.

'I'll give her such a talking to to-morrow as will put this nonsense out of her head,' he said to himself furiously. His impulse was to go then and there and administer the 'talking-to,' but the fresh air—he had gone out on the lawn—calmed his excitement. He reflected that his arrival at the Rectory at that moment, in a towering passion, to scold the young lady of the house, would probably give rise to some comment. He therefore deferred action till the morrow.

The morrow came, but it brought a telegram from his brother, necessitating his instant departure for London on important business. He had to set out by the first train, being thus compelled to defer the 'talking-to,' but he hoped to return the following day, and nothing important could be done by her in that short time.

CHAPTER X.

Before going to bed that night Audrey metaphorically smoked a pipe of peace with Harold Carew.

'I did not mean to sneer at your friend,' he said as he was bidding her good-night. 'I would not have done so on any account. I fully appreciate her courage. Indeed, I did not think—' hesitating.

She finished the sentence. 'You did not think her capable of coming to such a decision or of carrying it out.'

'I know very little of her,' he urged in a defensive tone. 'My mother is enthusiastic about her; and, be assured, I meant nothing disparaging when I said I did not think her fit to be a governess. If you will mention my suggestion to her, it may be of use. I wonder something of the sort has not already occurred to her.'

'Am I to tell her you think she might succeed as a writer of flippant articles on serious subjects?' she asked, laughing.

He smiled a little. 'You take my words too literally; but you may put my suggestion in any form you please, so as you make it. It is worth attending to, believe me.'

Audrey did mention the suggestion to her friend, drawing from her the confession that it had been anticipated.

Audrey was in raptures.

'You must consult Claude,' she said. 'He knows all about that sort of thing, and is the proper person to help you.'

Laura's face assumed a look of sensitive shrinking, as if from some painful contact.

'I would rather not tell Claude,' she answered hastily; 'he might not like it.'

'Not like it! He would be delighted, which is more than he is at the thought of your being a governess, I can tell you.'

'What did he say about that?' in a tone of apparent indifference.

'Not much, but he looked all the more. This is a different thing, and you are sure to succeed. It is so odd Harold Carew should have thought of it.'

'It is rather nice of him, considering how I have snubbed him,' said Laura, laughing.

Audrey overruled all her objections to telling Claude, refusing to entertain for a moment the supposition that he could dislike such a course.

While the two girls were sitting together the Ellises called, and Laura, as variable as the wind, was soon engaged in gay *persiflage* with St. Clare Ellis, who was gifted with the faculty of always attaching himself to the most amusing lady in the company.

He gave one the idea of having run to beard, for all his hair had left the top of his head and transferred itself to his chin, where it flourished in rich luxuriance. The part of his face which was visible was marked by the good-tempered geniality characteristic of the Ellis family.

Mr. Carew, who had come out to recreate

himself a little after his severe studies, stood watching them for some time in silence; then addressing Sir Digby—

'Who could think for a moment that that girl is fit to be a governess? Look at her now.'

The baronet apparently saw nothing remarkable in her demeanour; for after a pause he said, more in answer to his own thoughts than to Harold's remark,

'The time to see her in perfection is with Claude; if he chaffs her, for example, over a game of croquet, when her dress gets in the way of her mallet.'

Claude Dashwood's name always had a discomposing effect on Harold. On hearing it, lately especially, the usual sarcastic expression of his face deepened into a kind of sardonic gloom. On this occasion he was, no doubt, disgusted at the idea of a sane masculine human being playing croquet when he might have been improving his mind.

Claude returned from London just in time for dinner, and the moment that important event was over, his sister, clasping her hands over his arm, led him out on the terrace and communicated her secret, eagerly claiming his help and sympathy.

She was by no means prepared for the look of fierce anger that crossed his face the moment he took in her meaning.

'That's Carew!' he exclaimed in a tone of concentrated jealousy.

'Carew! Why, my dear, she has written the story, and she could not have done that in two days.'

'I hate literary women,' he said wrathfully. 'Unless she gives up such a scheme, I wash my hands of her altogether. It is the very height of absurdity. What can she know to write about? She has never been anywhere.'

In vain Audrey pleaded her friend's cause. Claude would listen to no reason. He launched a fierce philippic against blues and strong-minded ladies; urged the general incompetency of women; inveighed against their writing as weak poor stuff, the prevalence of which had vitiated the public taste; and ended by wishing there were some stringent law which would prevent their ever printing a line.

Audrey was astounded. Bitterly regretting that she had not been guided by Laura's advice, she tried to mitigate his anger by dwelling on the motive which had prompted her friend.

'Even the motive does not reconcile me to it,' he returned angrily.

Audrey was too deeply hurt to reply. For the first few moments she felt almost stunned by his ungenerous, even brutal, reception of an appeal made to him in the full confidence of perfect trust.

The conviction that she had injured Laura in his estimation added to her distress. She sat silent for some time, then,

'I am so sorry I told you anything about it,' she said at last. 'Laura wanted me not to do so. She was afraid you would not like it.'

'She was, was she? Then why did she do it?'

'Claude, you speak as though you were engaged to her, and had a right to dictate to her.' He was silent, and she went on: 'It is imperative that she should do something. You would equally dislike her being a governess.'

'John is the person to work, not Laura.'

'Only he can't or won't. They are doing their best to get him something; but I have no faith in him.'

'And she is to work for the family? A nice project!' contemptuously.

A long pause.

'Then won't you do anything to help us, Claude?' resumed his sister tremulously.

'I would rather cut my hand off than help in such a cause.'

'I gave you credit for more generosity. Had any one told me such a thing of you, nothing would have induced me to believe it. I should have thought affection for me, to say nothing of Laura, whom you have known ever since she was a baby, would have made you act differently.'

'I will speak to Laura about it myself to-morrow.'

'I beg you will do nothing of the sort. She very unwillingly consented to my consulting you, and as you decline to help her, spare her at least the violent tirade you have treated me to.'

She went indoors, more angry with him than she had ever been in her life before.

She was not more angry than he was. She had made him feel, somehow, that he was 'a brute,' and if there was one conviction Claude Dashwood disliked having forced on him more than another, it was that. Had he been consulted at the creation, as he always felt he ought to have been, he would certainly have dissuaded the Creator from bestowing on woman that potent and most diabolic faculty whereby she at times convicts her tormentor—protector, helpmate, whatever he is—of unmitigated brutality.

Unable to enjoy his cigar in any degree of peace, he went up to his sister's room, to try again whether he could not bring her round to his way of thinking. He failed to do so.

'I did not think you could be so ungenerous,' was her only answer to his remarks.

'Well, look here, Audrey, I frankly confess I hate the whole thing; but as you have set your heart on it I will look over this precious story, and see if anything can be done with it.'

'Certainly not,' proudly. 'With your ideas you could not be a fair judge. I will help my friend now without your assistance, and even if it should all end in failure, I shall always admire her for having tried to do something to assist her father and mother. I think it is quite splendid of her, and if you had a spark of the generosity I credited you with, you would see that it is, instead of talking nonsense about vitiating the public taste.'

'I will be as impartial as any one can be. Let me have it, Audrey.'

She declined, and he left her, much aggrieved at her 'obstinacy.'

The Irish element preponderated largely in Audrey, and she shared to the fullest extent one characteristic of the genuine Irishwoman, viz. an altogether instinctive feeling that she had an inherent right, in virtue of her sex, to the help and assistance of men. This characteristic of Irishwomen is the result probably of the nature of Irish chivalry—an essentially different thing from its English equivalent. An Englishman is chivalrous because women are weak; but the consideration due to weakness is always tinged, to a certain extent, with the contempt felt by him for it; nor is he ever quite free from some portion of the feeling expressed by the excellent St. Chrysostom when he pronounces woman 'a necessary evil; a natural temptation; a desirable calamity; a domestic peril; a deadly fascination; and a painted ill.'

An Irishman's chivalry, on the contrary, is the unconscious yet genuine expression of his conviction that woman is the crowning work of creation, and that the world would be simply unendurable without her. And this difference influences the women of the respective nations. The Irishwoman accepts with pride that which she knows to be given ungrudgingly; while the Englishwoman is rather apt to despise in her heart that which, being accorded to her supposed weakness only, has so large an element of contempt in it.

In accordance with this feeling, Audrey had expected her brother's coöperation and assistance in anything she took in hand as a matter of right. Her resentment at his reception of her request was extreme. It would be hard to say whether she felt more anger, surprise, or pain. 'Even if he disliked it, he ought to have done it because I asked him.' That was her old-fashioned and very Hibernian view of the matter.

How was she to break the news to Laura? 'She will be so hurt,' was her thought; for she naturally judged her friend's sensations by her own.

CHAPTER XI.

It would be unfair not to sympathise with Claude in his annoyance with Laura. In the first place, the dislike felt by a certain type of man for a woman capable of the least intellectual exertion is really instinctive. He cannot help it, and is not to be blamed for it. But, setting that aside, he had other grounds of complaint. To initiate a career for herself in that independent way was surely a great piece of feminine presumption?

Had she relieved her impecuniosity by selling herself openly for money to some Crœsus with one foot in the grave and the other bandaged up for the gout, he would not have been half so angry; he would, in such a case, have judged her leniently, making allowance for her circumstances; but a girl who could conceive the idea of writing a book and carry it out, and who could, farther, propose leaving her home to become a governess, had in her potentialities for any amount of strongmindedness; and none such, unless she renounced her evil ways, should enjoy the perilous distinction of being his wife.

But he was not without hopes that she would renounce her evil ways, though he was unable to administer that 'talking to' which he had meditated on the following day.

Fretting about John's debts, grief at the prospect of leaving her home, and anxiety to know the result of Audrey's communication to Claude, brought on one of the bad headaches to which Laura was subject, and for which a day in bed was the only remedy.

When, therefore, her irate lover called to see her, he was met by the intelligence that she would be invisible to him till to-morrow, at least. The disappointment did not add to the serenity of his temper, nor were matters improved by his getting back just in time to hear Harold Carew ask Audrey if she had imparted his suggestion to her friend.

Being informed that she had done so, he inquired what Miss Erle had said.

'That it was very kind of you to interest yourself in her, especially considering how you had both quarrelled.'

'*I* did not quarrel,' in a voice of injured innocence. 'She attacked me violently every time she saw me. It was her doing entirely.'

'Little flirt!' muttered Claude, between his teeth, prefacing the words by an adjective, reprehensible perhaps, but relieving to his feelings. 'Have you seen Laura?' he asked his sister.

'Yes; only for a minute, though; her head was so bad she could hardly speak.'

'I suppose you told her all I said?' a little anxiously.

'No, not all. I told her the general drift. I had to do so.'

He looked annoyed.

'What did she say?'

'Not much; she was too ill.'

'Thought me brutal and ungenerous, of

course. Women always do, if you say a word they don't like.'

'Your opinion of their powers is such, that I should imagine it mattered little to you what they thought.'

Uneasy at the effect his conduct might have on Laura, he launched into a violent defence of himself and his opinions, and ended by renewing his request to see the manuscript.

This was refused. In the short consultation the two girls had had that morning, they had resolved that, whatever they did henceforth, they would do for themselves. Their one application for help had ended so unfortunately, that they would not make a second. Both were proud and sensitive—Laura was especially so on this point—and would not subject themselves to another repulse.

Audrey had said something about consulting Harold Carew.

Laura would not hear of it.

'After all,' she observed, 'if one wants really to do a thing, one must help one's self.

It is no use trusting to other people. I did think John might have been of some use, but he is so afraid. Now, I will just act for myself. You would feel as I do, Audrey, if you had seen papa and mamma this morning when the post came in, bringing a bill a yard long, for Charlie's school expenses.'

But though Laura had resolved to act for herself, she suffered acutely from the consciousness that she was doing so in opposition to Claude's wishes. His disapproval took the life out of all her efforts, and her unhappiness was increased by feeling that perhaps she ought not to care whether he liked what she did or not. She could not deny to herself that whether she ought or ought not to do so, she did actually care very much. It was unaccountable that Claude had not come and spoken to her himself. It is true she had tried to avoid him, but a certain instinct told her that he could easily have found her had he made any resolute effort to do so. She had no thought now about his asking her to be his wife. If he would only have said, 'All right, Laura; I didn't like the idea at first, but I see all you mean about it, and whether you win or lose, we shall be none the less friends,' she would have been quite happy.

Claude Dashwood had a horrible temper; he was jealous and touchy, and would make the misery of any woman who married him, but he was not bad-hearted, and had he known the full extent of all he made Laura suffer at this time, he would have been deeply shocked. The truth was, that he had fallen in love with, and won the love of a girl whose nature he was utterly unable to appreciate, or, indeed, understand. He saw one side of her only, the side naturally most prominent during her girlhood, made more prominent too by the fact that she was personally exceedingly graceful and attractive, and consequently much sought after; while her volatile manner, her gaiety, her innocent readiness for any amount of dancing, flirting, amusement, and 'fun'—all the result of youthful high spirits —blinded him to the indications of graver character which showed themselves plainly enough in her domestic life. He could not see that something deeper lay beneath. His violent prejudices, too, obscured his judgment; for only the most cruel prejudice could have been blind to the fact that, though filial affection was the immediate motive actuating her, a something stronger than herself was struggling in her for utterance. There was a dash of genius in her causing that innate restlessness, that perpetual straining after some vague ideal, which tormented her.

In all this Claude had no intention whatever of being unkind. He followed the dictates of his own nature as she followed hers. But though she followed these dictates, she did it, so to speak, under protest. Claude's influence over her was great though not supreme, and it had always tended to make her ashamed of the powers she felt unconsciously that she possessed. He repressed every manifestation of originality and cleverness on her part as ruthlessly as Mrs. Elliott cut down, in her geometrical garden, any aspiring flower daring to lift its head above the crowded level of its fellows. The girl suffered very acutely from this. It was the 'rift within the lute' which marred all the happiness of her intercourse with him. She was painfully sensible of a want of mental liberty in his society, and though she tried involuntarily to keep herself down to the standard she knew he liked, she was secretly restless and dissatisfied.

CHAPTER XII.

WHILE the minds of Claude and Laura were being thus exercised by the attempts of the latter towards an independent career, the great social event of the neighbourhood was a picnic of magnificent proportions, by which Mrs. Ellis proposed inaugurating her daughters' autumn campaign. There had been at first some doubt as to where it should take place. Several localities had been named as eligible spots on which to learn to bear discomfort cheerfully, and make an involuntary study of entomology. Finally, Sir Digby Forester settled the matter by proposing that Glynton should be the scene of the festivities. Mrs. Ellis was delighted. Whether the offer resulted from the gentleman's instantaneous conversion to the charms of Miss Violet, or from mere good nature, was a matter of comparative indifference. The thing was that he had made it, and what scope did it not afford for the piscatory efforts of the six Miss Ellises?

It always rains, or it is very hot, or there is an east wind on the day fixed for a picnic. On this particular day it was very hot, so hot that none but English people would have thought of taking their pleasure under such a scorching sun.

Harold Carew had left Enleigh, but Lady Emily was still there, and she and Audrey and Digby started early for Glynton to avoid the great heat.

The thought that they must meet on this day was the one uppermost in the minds of Claude and Laura from the moment the affair had been decided on. On learning that he was going, the girl's impulse had been to decline doing so herself, but a little reflection showed her that such a course would bring on her a world of wondering comment and inquiry.

Mrs. Elliott, thinking Claude had started

with Audrey and Lady Emily, sent down to the Rectory to say she would drive Mrs. Erle and Laura over to Glynton. She had not offered to do so till she had heard that her nephew was gone, for she never willingly afforded him and Laura an opportunity of being together.

The latter, on hearing that the person who was incessantly in her thoughts had already left Enleigh, went up there with a feeling of relief. She dreaded the meeting with him so much that she accepted as a reprieve everything tending to delay it; and yet there was a pang—keen and sharp—mingled with the relief. A short time before, Claude would have driven her over to Glynton himself, or ridden with her, overruling her objections to going about all day in her habit. In those little matters she had been so proud of having her objections overruled by him. She always began by objecting; which afforded him an opening for one of the lectures so dear to the hearts of men, though they deny the fact. In return for the lecture, she would contradict him and laugh at him; but in these small conflicts he invariably came off victor — for the best of all reasons, that his antagonist was willing to be vanquished.

Both Mrs. Elliott and Laura were mistaken in thinking Claude had started. He had not; having avoided doing so in the hope of seeing the young lady, and coming to an understanding with her. He had made up his mind to offer himself as her husband. That would be a solution of all her difficulties, would obviate the necessity for those exertions on her part which grated so painfully on his prejudices; and in no other way could he hope to regain his own peace of mind, now fatally disturbed. He had tried that week to do without seeing her, to put her out of his thoughts. In vain; her gay joyous face, with its flitting expressions of tenderness, her sweet young voice, haunted him perpetually. The colour seemed taken out of his life when he heard no longer the laughing careless criticisms on every one and everything.

But though compelled to acknowledge

that he could not do without her, he was angry both with himself and with her. He disliked feeling that his hand had been forced. He disliked feeling that her capacities and prospects had been openly discussed. He disliked feeling that he had given her pain, and might have to give her more, for he meant to attach a condition to his proposal. If she became his wife, she must renounce, at once and for ever, all attempts at authorship.

At the anticipation of seeing her he had worked himself up into a fever of impatience.

He was not on the spot when she arrived, and only saw her first when she was sitting under the cedar-tree engaged in telling a story to little Eveleen, Charlie's child, who remained at Enleigh during her parents' absence abroad. Looking up suddenly, she perceived him coming across the lawn towards her. Excessive surprise at this unexpected sight so overcame her, that for a moment she became almost unconscious of what she was doing. In her nervousness she addressed some words to the child beside her, and stooping, kissed her forehead with a caressing movement of her hand over her long hair.

Claude chose to believe that this perfectly innocent, almost unconscious, action was done with some reference to himself. One of the things he most frequently told his sister was, that her friend was 'a most consummate and finished coquette'—an imputation always strenuously denied by Audrey. And justly so; for Laura was certainly not a finished coquette, if by that term be meant one who makes coquetry an art and study. There was, nevertheless, a great deal of natural and very innocent coquetry in her, as there is in every woman who is conscious of her power to attract and fascinate. Numbers of women are totally unconscious of this power, if they are endowed with it; but Laura was not one of these.

She could not help being aware that, without any effort on her part, men were attracted by her—sometimes even against their will—as was Harold Carew. No one was more susceptible to this subtil influence exercised by her than Claude. Not content, however, with acknowledging the natural power which she undoubtedly possessed, he was wont to attribute to her all sorts of elaborate and—in the estimation of an honourable woman—not very creditable devices for the further assertion of her supremacy. He did not condemn her for these (supposed) devices. They were, he considered, a woman's legitimate weapons. They had 'man' for their object, and were, he believed, totally incompatible with that strong-mindedness, which was far worse in his eyes than vice or crime.

But though, as a rule, he would not have condemned Laura for using such weapons, he resented, on this especial occasion, that which he considered a challenge. His feeling towards her at the moment trembled in the balance between intense hate and fierce love, or the thing he called such; and there was as much anger as courtesy in the tone in which he accosted her.

'How do you do, Laura? It is so long since I have seen you, that I began to think we were never to meet again.'

A blinding sensation came over her as she gave her hand, responsive to the one he held out, in a somewhat imperious way. He retained it in a firm grasp.

'Come with me; I want to speak to you,' raising her from her seat.

Freeing her hand, she accompanied him in silence. He turned down a shady walk leading to a small flower-garden, surrounded with high walls, called the Lady's Garden.

'Laura,' he began, when they got near it, 'why have you avoided me? Why have you kept out of my way for the last week?'

'I didn't—I mean—I don't know,' she stammered.

'Yes, you did,' he interrupted impetuously, 'and I have thought it very unkind of you.'

'Why didn't you come and see me?' she retorted, with reviving courage.

'You know very well I did, and that you persistently refused to see me,' which was only partially true.

They had reached the steps leading down

to the old-fashioned garden. She hesitated, as if doubting whether to go on or not.

'What do you want to say to me, Claude?' she asked, an indication of haughty resentment in her voice. 'If you speak to me in that way, I won't go on with you.'

He suddenly put his arm round her waist, almost lifting her down the steps, and bending over her, covered her face with kisses.

Intense anger gave her strength to free herself from his detaining grasp.

'Claude, how could you dare? What could induce you?' she exclaimed, her eyes flashing indignant scorn at him. 'Are you mad?'

Her anger brought back his reason, and with it a keen sense of shame. For a moment he could not answer, and she turned towards the house. He placed himself before her quickly.

'Laura, stop—I beg of you—I apologise—listen to me—'

'Let me pass; you must be out of your senses,' tears of outraged delicacy filling her eyes.

'I cannot let you pass, Laura, till you have heard what I have to say to you. I thought you would understand—you must understand—surely no words are needed between us. I want you to be my wife; I thought you knew that, or I should not—not have ventured. Give me your hand, Laura;' and he drew a step nearer.

She dashed the angry tears from her eyes.

'I wish you hadn't done that,' she said.

'I was so sure you understood what I meant,' in an apologetic way, and trying to take her hand, but gently, as if afraid of alarming her again.

'How was I to know?' she asked. 'I had no idea what—what you were going to say. I thought you wanted to speak about something very different,' with a burning blush.

'We'll come to that presently,' he answered. 'I wanted to speak about a great many things; but first'—drawing her towards him—'you know what I mean now? I can't think how you ever doubted it.'

'You are always telling me I jump to conclusions,' she returned, smiling a little through her tears; 'but that was a conclusion you might have been very sure I should not have jumped to without sufficient grounds.'

'Well, now that you know your grounds, what is your conclusion?' he asked, smiling in his turn, and putting his arm round her.

'That you shouldn't take things for granted in that—that exceedingly premature way.'

They sat down on an iron seat near, and he lavished on her a volume of tender epithets and caresses, claiming from her in return some expression of her affection for him.

She looked at him for a moment out of her clear fearless eyes, and then, murmuring some scarcely intelligible words, suddenly hid her face on his shoulder.

They sat for some time in silence, till the sun, chasing the shadows before it, drove them away. Then they walked up and down the broad path in the shade cast by the elms growing on the other side of the wall. A light wind was rustling the leaves in the tree-tops, and now and again the wood-pigeons called to each other in notes of tender softness.

Laura was tall, so that her lover could walk with his arm round her waist without inconvenience to either, and she, at least, had some seconds of perfect happiness, as he bent over her with soft words and passionate caresses.

But no perfect happiness lasts. Laura's did not. Sensitive to every change in Claude's expression, in his tone, she speedily became aware of a look of non-content in his face.

His features were like Audrey's; there was in them the same regular high-bred cast—the same thick straight eyebrows—the same gray eyes, large, and looking black at times. Both had a particularly beautiful smile. Claude's quite redeemed his face, the expression of which—to a stranger—was not prepossessing, though he was very handsome. But Laura, in the smile which his moustache did not conceal, and in the gray eyes bent on her now with a look of triumphant love, saw something which told her that he was not fully satisfied in his mind. Deeply sensible of the disparity of their condition—he with so much to bestow, and she so little—she feared that some doubt as to how his family would receive the announcement of his engagement was troubling him.

'Claude,' she said, looking at him, 'you have made my happiness, but it is a dreadfully bad match for you; it is really a case of the church mouse with me—you know that, don't you?'

He answered by a smile and a reassuring caress, which, however, failed to satisfy her. She still felt a vague sense of uneasiness. There was a reason for it. Claude's victory was only half won. He had not doubted Laura's ready acceptance of his offer. But he wanted something more. She must give up, henceforth and for ever, all idea of earning money in any way either for herself or others.

He never flinched from his determination to exact a promise to this effect from her; but he found it less easy than he had imagined to put his requisition into words.

It was one thing to make fierce resolutions in her absence—another to carry them into effect, walking with his arm round her waist—her beautiful face quivering beneath his glances with the sweet surprise of her first love.

He told himself again and again during that walk up and down, that he had a perfect right to impose this condition as the price of all he had to bestow. Claude was a little too conscious of all he had to bestow. The rich man who marries a penniless girl must be either a fool or a hero, if he is not conscious, to a certain extent, that he is the one who gives most—as giving is usually understood; but, then, this consciousness should not be always present with him—it should not be constantly in his mind—and it is not, if he is generous. If it is, there is small chance of happiness for the girl he marries. He will be continually weighing what he has given, and thinking he has never had enough in return.

Claude was not ungenerous as a rule; but the secret shame he could not help feeling at what he was about to do made him try to justify himself in his own eyes by dwelling on the substantial equivalent he had it in his power to make for the concession he meant to demand. Still he was at a loss how to put his requisition, nor did Laura's next remark lessen the difficulty of his task.

Seeing that something was still wrong,

'Claude, if you spoke on an impulse, not having weighed well what you did, it is not too late to retract. It is, as I daresay Mrs. Elliott has told you, a serious thing to marry a penniless girl like me, and I would rather the whole thing came to an end at once than feel you ever regretted, even for a moment, what you had done.'

As she spoke she freed herself from his arm, and looked at him with fearless frankness.

'I shall never regret it, my dearest, never. What put such an idea into your head?' placing his arm round her again firmly.

'I thought you looked uncertain, somehow, as if you were not satisfied. What is it, Claude? I would rather know.'

'There is a subject, Laura, on which I must speak to you,' bending over her so that she could not see his face. 'I hope Audrey told you how much I appreciated and admired your wish to do something to help your father,' hesitatingly, as if uncertain how he should proceed.

She looked at him gravely for a minute, then smiled a little as she answered,

'She certainly did not. As I understood the matter, you did not either appreciate or admire it; but you see, Claude, it was a case of necessity with me. The church mouse mayn't be able to do much in the way of making a fortune; but you shouldn't blame him for trying, at least,' with a deepening colour.

'But it will no longer be a case of the church mouse, Laura, I'm happy to say: I'm not a millionaire, but I have enough for both of us; so you must promise me never to think of anything of the sort again.'

It was not so much his words as the tone in which he spoke that jarred on her, in spite of the caress with which he tried to soften his meaning.

'Think of what?' she asked rather abruptly.

'Well, Laura, I shouldn't care to see you write or do anything of that kind now.'

'And you want me to promise not?' she asked, with inconvenient directness.

Claude wished she would have given the promise without forcing him to express himself so openly on the subject.

'I feel sure there is no need for any promise, dear. I know you will be always ready to meet my wishes; still, to avoid misunderstanding—' He paused, as if expecting a ready assent from her; but no assent came, and they walked to the end of the path and back again in silence.

Laura felt a sudden glow of anger, combined with a deep sense of pain, at this attempt to bargain with her. It was as though he was offering her so much money for her mental liberty. And if she sold herself, how were John's debts to be kept from his father's knowledge?

'Well, darling?' he said at last, thinking she had had ample time to consider the matter.

'I should not like to make any promise about it,' she replied, in rather a low voice.

'Why not?' he exclaimed, his temper roused, as it always was at the least opposition.

'Because I don't think you have any right to ask it.'

'As to right, Laura, where there is affection there should be no question of right.'

'Nor of bargain either, Claude,' she retorted rather haughtily.

'Bargain! It is not bargaining to say what I wish.'

'But, you see, my wishes count for something too; only that is a little fact you seem to have forgotten.'

'I have not forgotten it,' he returned; 'but if you have the feeling for me you confessed to just now, you should have no difficulty in acceding to my request.'

His arm was still round her waist, but all the soft light was gone out of his eyes, and an expression of hard determination deepening on his face.

'Am I to understand that you make this promise a condition of our engagement—our marriage, in fact?' she asked, again with that inconvenient directness, and freeing herself from his arm.

'That is not the way to put it, Laura;' and commanding his rising temper he said gently enough that she was mistaken in supposing he did not do justice to her wish to help her parents. He did, most fully; but henceforth there would be no need for any independent effort on her part, as he would willingly coöperate in all plans she might form for their benefit, and that he considered he was, under the circumstances, justified in asking her to promise not to engage in a pursuit which he distinctly disliked and disapproved of. 'In all constitutional governments, you know, the subjects make terms with their sovereign,' he concluded, with a smile meant to be reassuring.

'And the sovereign has it in his power to reject the terms,' she answered gently. 'Besides, you mistake altogether, Claude. I never thought of asking you or wanting you to do anything to—to—help any one belonging to me,' in a surprised pained way, and flushing deeply. 'Neither they nor I would trespass on your kindness in such a manner as that. Such an idea would never have entered my head.'

She meant that help which would have come gracefully and naturally from her would be totally inadmissible from him.

He put his arm round her again.

'You little atom of independence! There will be no trespassing in the matter. You will have a house in London, where you will reign as a queen—and a very beautiful and graceful queen you will be—and I will be your first subject. You will have your own carriage to drive about in, and, of course, you will have your father and mother, and John and Amy, and any mortal soul you please, to stay with you.'

Clearly he was of Geraint's opinion, that to secure a woman's affections you need only dress her beautifully.

The picture was a tempting one to a girl who had lived in an atmosphere where every slight indulgence, every infinitesimal pleasure, was a matter for grave consideration. She knew, too, that the picture would probably be realised. Claude was generosity itself, so far as money was concerned. He would, she was certain, be lavishly indulgent to her.

'Now won't that satisfy you?' he went on. 'I will be a very loyal and tractable subject, Laura, though you may not think it because I insist on this one concession.'

But she was not satisfied, though he tried to win her by a profusion of caresses. Her sensation was one of profound humiliation. She felt that it was ungenerous of him to exact a promise she was not willing to give; she did not think he had any right to ask a promise from her in the matter. She was but two-and-twenty—only just beginning to be conscious of her own powers. How could she bind herself by a vow never to use them, no matter how they developed themselves? Besides, if she precluded herself from the possibility of earning money in some way, how were John's debts to be paid? How was she to get a trousseau? This last may seem a prosaic consideration to romantic people who have never known anxiety as to the wherewithal; but Laura had been Miss Thoughtful all her short life; had shared her parents' burdens from the age of ten. She knew that trousseaux are not got for nothing; knew, too, how scanty was the store from which hers would have to be provided. If the double drain of her trousseau and John's debts came on that store at once, she was well aware that it would be unequal to the demand made on it, and then—what would be the effect on her father? She would have bought her own happiness at the expense of those with whom her very being was bound up. But she could not lay these difficulties before Claude. All the delicate instincts of her nature shrank from such a course.

The struggle in her mind showed itself plainly on her face, and Claude's keen eyes, fixed on her, added to her embarrassment.

'I cannot bind myself by any promise,' she said, after a pause.

He walked to the end of the path and back to where she stood; her face burning, her brown hair all in picturesque disorder from the way in which her head had been resting against his shoulder, her tall graceful figure in its white dress standing out against the background of trees and flowers. When he came up to her again she suddenly placed her hand on his arm.

'Claude, will you not trust me? Why do you act as if you had no confidence in me? I don't like the feeling that you want to make a bargain with me.'

He was moved in spite of his prejudice;

but a certain obstinacy of disposition, which prevented his admitting that he had ever been in the wrong, came like an evil angel between him and his better impulse.

It irritated him, too, to see that she was less pliable than he had conceived she would be in that first moment of his triumph and of her young love.

'You persist in talking about a bargain, Laura,' he began; 'but be reasonable. I offer you a home—'

'Pray don't give yourself the trouble to go over the items again,' she exclaimed, hurt at his persistance.

'Hear me out, Laura, before you reject my offer. I would provide you with a home, which I would do my best to make happy for you. You shall share all I have; I will deny you no luxury my means afford—'

'Except the luxury of being free—mentally free—I know all that is implied in the promise you want me to make—and of feeling that my husband trusts me. No, Claude; I have, as you know, not one farthing in the world; but I decline to sell my real self—the part of me that cannot die—for a house in London and a carriage. I reject your offer, with all the luxuries you speak of'—scornfully—'knowing their value, but valuing something else more. I can understand your thinking the thing I call my mind not worth such a sacrifice. Very likely it isn't. Still, "a poor thing, but mine own," you know, and I mean to keep it.'

'Very well; that ends the matter.'

That was Claude's answer, wrung from him by the bitter words she spoke, and the contempt he discerned both in her look and tone.

He turned and left the garden.

She stood for fully ten minutes without moving, almost without breathing, unconscious of everything save the one overwhelming conviction of Claude's narrowness, his want of generosity. The veil had been roughly torn from her eyes. 'To think that I would sell myself for a house and a carriage!' That was the only definite idea in her mind.

At last she threw herself on the iron seat, unheeding the sun, which was pouring his scorching rays down full on her head. Her pretty hair, her bright fresh dress, were all dishevelled and disarranged. As if in a dream, she heard her mother's voice calling her; but she made no more effort to answer the call than if she had not heard it. The whole outer world seemed a far-off thing, with which she had no concern. Reality was, for her, summed up in that aching sense of wounded pride gnawing at her heart.

CHAPTER XIII.

Meantime Claude, in a paroxysm of anger and disappointment, had gone back to the house. He turned into the dining-room, and sat there he knew not how long, till Eveleen's voice calling him disturbed him. To avoid her he went out through the window, but on the lawn he met Mrs. Erle.

'Do you know where Laura is?' she asked. 'No one can find her, and we ought to have started long ago.'

'I don't know where she is now. She was in the Lady's Garden.'

'Would you kindly see if you can find her? Mrs. Elliott is in despair.'

He was a little calmer by this time, and went in search of her.

She was still sitting on the iron seat when he reached the garden; but she heard his advancing step, and, starting up, stood gazing at him, with the alarmed yet defiant look of some graceful hunted creature driven to bay.

Though admiring her more than any woman he had ever seen, he had not thought her beautiful till that day. That she was so he admitted now with a pang of fierce anger.

'They are waiting for you,' he said, trying studiously to speak indifferently. 'Mrs. Erle asked me to come and tell you so.'

'You have not said anything to her?' she exclaimed eagerly.

'No.'

'I must beg you not to tell her anything; it will spoil her day, and she so seldom goes out.' She looked at him, expecting a negative promise.

'You have not given me any right to an interest in your affairs; but I can fully understand your dislike to letting your mother know the decision you have come to.'

She would not condescend to answer this.

'Don't wait; I will come presently,' she said, seeing that he still lingered.

He did not move, but stood watching her as she smoothed back her hair and put on her hat.

So much of fierce passion mingled with his regretful anger, that he had almost lost all control over himself. Something in his bearing and in his look warned the girl of this; calling to mind, as she did, his violent demonstration once before that morning.

'Go on, I will come afterwards,' she repeated imperiously, yet with the same defiant air, veiling the apprehension she felt.

Deeply incensed at her evident mistrust, he advanced a little way into the garden, thus leaving her free egress; taking off his hat, and bowing low, at the same time, as if to a complete stranger.

She went on rapidly, he following more slowly. Her whole soul was now bent on keeping her mother in ignorance of the affair. Any suspicion of it would, she knew, effectually spoil the brightness of her day.

Mrs. Erle was standing on the steps.

'Where *have* you been, Laura? Why, what is the matter? How flushed you look!'

she exclaimed, with that scrutinising maternal glance, compounded equally of criticism, anxiety, and affection, which daughters find so aggravating.

Laura was not more patient under the inspection than young ladies generally are.

'Nothing is the matter, mamma,' she replied unblushingly, though Mrs. Elliott's keen eye was on her; 'only it is very hot, and I came so quickly.'

'Have you a headache?' questioned the mother, who was in the habit of looking on her daughter's constitutional headaches as something between a crime and a misfortune. She always asked the question much as she would have asked, "Have you committed a murder? Let me know the worst.'

'No, mamma, of course I haven't,' responded the young lady, much as she would have repudiated the imputed crime.

Mrs. Erle attempted to arrange her hat, still directing on her that look of maternal scrutiny, as keen to detect a chance freckle as a latent heart-affection.

'Please don't, mamma,' said poor Laura, her embarrassment considerably increased by Claude's presence. Unable to let her out of his sight, he had come up, and was watching her with a dark gloomy look on his beautiful face. 'I will just go to Audrey's room and brush my hair,' she said, heedless of Mrs. Elliott's impatience; eager only to escape from her mother and her offended lover. If he meant to drive with them, and keep his eyes on her in that way, she did not know how she should get through the ordeal.

He, on his part, turned with a suppressed oath to find fault with the coachman for some fault in harnessing the horses. 'She can think of her hair at such a moment,' he muttered savagely.

He was hard to please. If she was not to cultivate her mind, it was surely allowable to brush her hair!

He had ordered his own dog-cart, meaning to drive her himself, had things taken the turn he wished. Now he started off alone.

This being the state of affairs between

them, it may be conceived that neither was in a happy frame of mind on arriving at Glynton. Claude's first impulse had been not to go there; his second, not to let Laura out of his sight. It was torture to him to think of her alone all that day, exposed to the attentions of other men.

Harold Carew, it is true, was absent, but there were Sir Digby Forester and St. Clare Ellis; and how might she not set herself to flirt with them, to avenge herself on him! She could not be with a man without flirting; that was his opinion of her; but maddening as the sight of her coquetries would be to him, some fascination drew him ever on to witness them.

Laura had succeeded, she hoped, in lulling her mother's suspicions. She talked and laughed incessantly during the drive.

Claude was eagerly questioned as to his tardy appearance. One glance sufficed to show Audrey that something had happened.

'What is the matter?' she whispered. 'Is Laura coming?'

'I believe so,' he answered briefly.

'I have quarrelled with Claude for ever,' was Laura's hurried explanation.

At luncheon he sat where he could see her. He watched with resentful anger her determined efforts to conceal all traces of agitation or disturbance; which efforts, he persisted in assuring himself, resulted, not from generous affection for her mother, but from heartless indifference. Once or twice their eyes met, drawn to each other's faces by an irresistible fascination.

Violet Ellis sat next to Claude, and to her he devoted himself; not ostentatiously, for that would, he conceived, have gratified Laura by showing his own mortification, but with sufficient zeal to transport that happy damsel with delight.

'I'm afraid Laura is not well,' said Mrs. Erle to Audrey uneasily. 'She has not eaten one morsel, and her face is so flushed.'

'She didn't complain to me,' replied Audrey evasively.

As soon as the two girls could do so unobserved they went away together, and Laura told her friend all that had taken place.

Audrey listened in dismay, expressing strong condemnation of her brother's conduct. 'But,' she concluded, 'when his anger cools down, and he has time to think over it all, he will see—'

'And do you think I would sell myself to him? Give up all I most value for a carriage and fine clothes and an opera-box? Yes, that was one of the bribes he held out. If I would promise not to unsex myself by using the faculties God gave me, he, Claude Dashwood, would give me an opera-box every year! I'm poor enough, God knows,' she ended, with a bitter laugh, 'but I would rather work my fingers to the very bone, or die of cold and hunger, and see those I love do the same, than accept luxury on such terms. And then to swear he loved me,' she resumed—'to swear it by every sacred thing he could think of! His love would be degradation. I'm glad I've quarrelled with him, Audrey.'

'O Laura, but think of him.'

'I can't help him. We should never have been happy together. I always felt when I was with him like that poor spirit whom some vile magician imprisoned till it went quite mad. The magician shut it up in a box, or some such thing, and it used to struggle and struggle and struggle to get out—I always was so sorry for it—and then some one came and released it. But if I let Claude imprison mine, only death could free it.'

'I didn't know you had that feeling towards him, dear.'

'Always; but I tried not to have it, because he was so kind to me—and—and—O Audrey, because I was a fool; but my eyes have been opened. I've eaten of the fruit of the tree of knowledge, and—well, I've learned something, of course'—with a sudden change of tone—'never to trust a man's oaths, for one thing. Don't be uneasy, Audrey. He will console himself speedily. Look at him now, talking to Violet Ellis just as a couple of hours ago he talked to me;' and her eyes turned to the spot where, under the arching trees, Claude was walking up and down with Violet, bending his handsome head to catch her words.

'She isn't troubled with such an unfeminine thing as a soul,' went on Laura. 'One cannot but wonder at the fatuity of the Almighty in having endowed some women with such inconvenient gifts. How can He so far have forgotten their natural sphere?'

'Laura dear!'

'I'm quite serious; and I do think Claude should send up a deputation, requesting that no more women with aspirations should be created for the annoyance and disquiet of men. Just look at the inconvenience I have put him to, all because God has made me what I am instead of—like Violet, for example. When Claude offers her a carriage and an opera-box, don't you suppose she will accept them gratefully?'

'Heaven forbid that he ever should!'

'When a man has such gifts to bestow, my dear Audrey, he is naturally anxious to find a recipient who will value him and them at their true worth. See, Claude is looking at us. Let us go back to the others, that he may not think we wish to disturb his tête-à-tête with the appreciative Violet.'

Audrey had never seen Laura in this mood before. Quite unable to offer any consolation in words, she could only look her sympathy, and trust that time would do something to allay the anger of both her and her lover.

Laura was right in saying that Violet would know how to appreciate Claude and the gifts he bore. She had left home that morning bent on enjoying herself. For once she would subordinate duty to pleasure, and give herself up to uninterrupted felicity, in the shape of a flirtation with Sir Digby Forester, who had met her friend, Colonel Wilmot, abroad, and with whom she proposed having a long conversation on the subject of that distinguished soldier.

But though bent on pleasure, Violet had a frugal mind; and when Claude, burning with anger against Laura, showed auspicious signs of readiness to prostrate himself at her own fair feet, she resolved heroically to deny herself the supreme gratification of a flirtation with the handsomest man in the company. This sacrifice involved another. She would be unable to satisfy that aching longing at her heart to hear about 'Dick Wilmot.' It was a bore, for she did want to hear about him, but he must not be allowed to interfere with serious business. He was very well in his way; very charming; and it was safe to flirt with him, precisely on the grounds which make it safe for a traveller to whistle before a highwayman. He had absolutely nothing, so could not expect even the most violent flirtation to end in matrimony. And Violet, who was strictly circumspect as to the men with whom she conversed, felt it a great boon to have on her list one member of the noble sex with whom she could be entirely at her ease.

But she abstained, though with regret, from mentioning Dick's name to Sir Digby;

abstained from more than a few passing words with the baronet himself. It was a sublime sacrifice of pleasure to duty, and the martyr felt herself distinctly elevated in the moral scale after she had resolved on it. She had her reward. Claude devoted himself to her all day. It would have been suicidal to damp his ardour.

Laura's breath came with such sharp spasms of pain, as she watched them, that she was almost suffocated. She had never before felt anything like the maddening sensation she experienced on seeing Claude help Violet into the match-boat, with all those marks of tender devotion which had hitherto been her own. It was her first real knowledge of the passion of jealousy, and it was not pleasant.

Then a sudden sense of shame—of the littleness of it all—came to her relief.

'How can I be such a fool as to care for a man whose ungenerous narrowness I can't help despising?'

In utter scorn of herself she asked this question, deriving some consolation for the moment from resolving to be superior both to him and to her lower self. It has been found, however, that philosophy is but a poor cure for love, even at the best of times.

Had Laura known it, the unconscious Violet was at that very instant driving Claude almost wild by the persistence with which she made her the subject of conversation.

Violet liked Laura. She amused and interested her, and she was not to be feared as a rival. A 'parson's' daughter, country bred and poor, could not compete with her, 'up' in all the latest requirements of a fashionable fisherwoman; and she thought her a safe subject to talk to Claude about, for, truth to tell, she did not find it very easy to get on with him.

They had not much in common. She could only talk about people, and that day Claude did not seem to know any one. He answered irrelevantly often enough till she mentioned Laura. Then he was all attention —such attention as the victim bestows on the executioner who is stretching him on the rack. The very sound of her name from indifferent lips was torture to him. He could praise and blame her himself, but he did not want to be reminded of her attractions, her bright ways and sunny face, by the first stranger he met.

He had missed her when she went away to speak to Audrey, and had been in a frenzy of anxiety about her. He looked round to see which man of the company was missing, but all were there, so she must, he thought, be alone. A compunctious stab went through his heart as he pictured her in tears, perhaps, and uncomforted. A sudden wild impulse seized him to rush after her, to scold her, scorn her, kiss her, anything so that he could see her, feel that she was still within his reach.

Then he saw her with Audrey, calm and collected apparently, but with a burning face and eyes unnaturally bright.

He knew her so well that he was sure she had a violent headache. He, as well as Mrs. Erle, had noticed that she had eaten nothing. Anything like physical suffering roused his deepest pity. On the headache of which she was almost unconscious he wasted sympathy which, had he accorded it to the real trials of her life, would have saved both infinite misery.

CHAPTER XIV.

When Audrey and Laura rejoined the party they found Sir Digby proposing that they should walk to the top of a neighbouring hill which commanded a splendid view of the surrounding country. The sun was going down, and a breeze having sprung up, exercise was not the impossibility it had been in the morning.

The hill rose almost to the dignity of a mountain. The road wound up between woods of larch, the delicate green of which contrasted beautifully with the darker hues of the forest trees beyond. The path was narrow and rocky; a mountain torrent frequently crossing it, and thereby interrupting the onward course of the pedestrians, and necessitating much assistance from the gentlemen to the ladies. Every foot of ground they passed was a world of beauty in itself. Up under the firs there was little save the rich carpet of moss, but the banks were thick with every variety of autumn flowers; rare ferns not easily to be found elsewhere here waved their graceful foliage, rejoicing in the congenial soil, and the streams abounding on all sides.

These streams had a charm peculiarly their own. They never gave an impression of damp. No doubt they did 'pay tribute to the genial heaven,' but the tribute went up in such delicate guise that no one was sensible it was being paid. They sparkled and danced over their rocky beds, clear and cold as crystal, stopping now and then to linger lovingly under some overhanging root, visiting a cool cavern where rare plants hid their exquisite loveliness, then tumbling in joyous haste over rocks and stones,

> 'Gliding and springing,
> . . . ever singing
> In murmurs as soft as sleep,'

they went till they came to a bit of smooth

reach, where they flowed on still rapidly but less noisily, letting you look into their clear depths, in which the many-coloured pebbles gleamed and glanced like jewels.

When they gained the first bit of level ground Digby bade them turn, and, having done so, such beauty met their eyes as, once seen, becomes 'a joy for ever.'

One of Nature's grand transformation scenes had taken place since the morning. The breeze had dispersed the golden haze, and the outline of the mountains stood out, unbroken, clearly defined against a sky of cloudless blue. Below dashed the river between precipitous banks, overhung with vegetation of every kind, from the tiny floweret up to the giant oak, as if to show that there was no form of beauty which the country could not produce.

'Isn't it grand?' said Digby to Audrey in a low voice, and taking off his hat unconsciously, as if in acknowledgment of Him who, in His strength, setteth fast the mountains. They all stood silent for some time, watching the shifting lights. Even the thoughtless Violet did momentary homage to the Eternal Perfection revealed in that glorious landscape.

On the homeward journey the party got separated, Claude, still with Violet under his wing, leading one detachment, including, amongst others, Laura, who, having got into conversation with Lady Emily and Mrs. Ellis, found herself drawn on after him.

One of the frequent mountain streams, flowing straight across their road, brought them to a standstill. The large rough stone forming the bridge had got so displaced that it was not easy for the ladies to cross without getting wet. A little higher up the stream there was a plank, but to reach it, it was necessary to get over an awkward stile into an adjoining field. However, to avoid the risk of being assisted by Claude, who was contemplating lifting the ladies over, Laura went into the field. Lady Emily and Mrs. Ellis followed her example. The stile was formidable, but it was not so bad as it would be to trust their precious persons to Claude and St. Clare Ellis. Of the latter Lady Emily expressed extreme distrust to Laura.

'I know what young men are!' she observed contemptuously. 'He is capable of dropping me into the middle of the stream and saying he did it by accident;' the truth being that he would not have been capable of lifting her at all, in spite of her long walks and sparing diet.

Violet and one or two other girls stayed with Claude, who assisted or lifted them over the water, much to his own and their satisfaction.

But Laura had not foreseen that after the stream was crossed another obstacle in the shape of a stile of most portentous form and size barred their return into the right road, and to her dismay, when she reached it, there was Claude, keeping guard, waiting to assist the party over—a look of triumph on his beautiful face indicating plainly how fully aware he was that he had circumvented her.

The stile was a break-neck device, a real

invention of the enemy—in fact, it was not a stile at all; it was a good stiff fence, formed of unbarked stems of young trees, necessitating all sorts of abnormal motions to enable one to reach the top, and still more monstrous proceedings to bring one to the bottom again in safety; not to mention the fact that when the fence was crossed there was still a tolerably steep bank to descend; nothing of a jump to young limbs, but presenting formidable difficulties to those excellent matrons before named. They looked, indeed, quite aghast, and reproached Laura in moving terms for having misled them. They even took counsel together as to whether it might not be better to go back and ford the stream, or trust themselves to Claude's arms, rather than risk life and limb by attempting to cross such an erection. They gazed wildly round for a more easy exit—for a gate or a less formidable barrier, but none presenting itself, Mrs. Ellis looked imploringly at her son; Lady Emily vainly wished for her dear Harold, and felt much inclined to scream.

It is sad to have to relate that Mrs. Ellis detected her son in the very act of exchanging looks of amusement with 'the demon Claude,' as Laura, in retailing the story afterwards to Audrey, disrespectfully termed her whilom lover. The said 'demon's' face wore a look of proud satisfaction. An opportunity was about to present itself for overpowering his contumacious ladye-love with a quite superior display of *force majeure*. She, assuredly, could not have lifted Mrs. Ellis over a high fence, but if she saw him bear with ease in his arms this gigantic humanity, how would she not feel the absurdity of her pretensions? What was the thing she fatuously called her mind compared to the sinewy arms capable of such a feat?

But with this triumphant prevision of making her acknowledge herself nowhere, there mingled a horrible fear of possible failure, together with a humiliating consciousness that he *wished* to shine in her eyes, and an altogether inferior and weak dread of her very pronounced turn for ridicule. Delightful would it be to lift that feminine Atlas on his shoulders, crushing by the sight his audacious enemy; but suppose he failed to lift the Atlas? or collapsed ignominiously under the attempt?

In spite of Laura's misery—and he, who read her face like a book, knew that she was intensely miserable—he was fully aware that no suffering could repress her diabolic sense of the ludicrous.

How would not her curved coral lips quiver with laughter, her bright eyes sparkle and dance with fun, if she saw him stagger backward and fall to the ground under the superincumbent weight of Mrs. Ellis's charms! Discretion is the better part of valour. He would not risk his reputation. He would abandon the attempt to crush Laura by any display of physical force, and would submit to be helped by St. Clare Ellis.

He secretly cherished the belief that Laura had no suspicion of all that was in his mind. Never was a belief more erroneous. That inconveniently clear-sighted young woman read his face as correctly as he read hers, and was perfectly aware of the nature of his thoughts.

'Will you help Mrs. Ellis down, or how, St. Clare?' asked Claude.

'Well, yes,' responded that distinguished warrior. 'How shall we manage? It is a tough place for the ladies.'

'Captain Ellis,' said Laura, speaking *over* Claude, 'there is a log of wood close by that oak-tree. If you would bring it across, Mrs. Ellis could step on it, and so get down more easily.'

'Capital! That's a clever thought of yours, Miss Erle;' and with a running leap he vaulted in the most finished manner over the fence. The ladies admired, as he expected them to do, his athletic powers, and the matrons all thanked Laura warmly for her timely suggestion.

'As I brought you here, it is well I should contrive some way out of the dilemma,' returned the young lady gravely.

Their descent being facilitated by the intervention of the log, they got over with comparatively little inconvenience.

Claude experienced a fresh access of anger against Laura. The quiet way in which she had ignored him mortified him extremely; nevertheless he stood by the fence still, assisting every one courteously enough. She waited till the last, hoping he would move; as he did not, she had no alternative but to face him. But she would not accept his help; at that moment she would have risked any personal danger rather than touch his hand.

When he held it out to aid her descent, she looked at him for an instant, her eyes full of indignant yet half-tender reproach, her lip curved with an expression of mingled pride and outraged dignity, and then jumped down unassisted. St. Clare sprang forward.

'What a jump! Have you hurt yourself? You might have sprained your ankle!'

'Not at all! I always manage better alone.'

Her eyes met those of Claude defiantly. The incident filled up the measure of his wrath. She was bent on defying him, and he bitterly congratulated himself on his escape from such a combination of pride and passion, one which any man might well hesitate to take to his heart.

Before they got home that evening, so certain did Violet feel that she had caught a fish, that she began to think how she could most judiciously shorten line preparatory to landing him.

CHAPTER XV.

'ALL I ask is that papa and mamma may not be told.' That was Laura's last remark to Audrey when they parted. The latter, as they drove home, turned over anxiously in her mind what course could most prudently be adopted. That the quarrel could be permanent, she would not for a moment admit. Something must be done to reconcile them; and she bethought herself of every argument likely to soften Claude.

She would dwell on Laura's disinterestedness. That he would surely appreciate even in his anger. She was mistaken. He did not appreciate it at all. Had she accepted his offer on his own terms, trusting to after-influence or contrivance for securing her own way, he, who felt almost loathing for her honest refusal to make a promise which she held that he had no right to exact, and doubted her ability to keep, would hardly have condemned the subterfuge, had she stooped to employ it. He would have made some cynical remarks about feminine want of sincerity and a woman's faculty for getting her own way in the end, and would have accepted the facts, believing evasion and shifty dealings to be her natural, almost her legitimate, weapons, of which man was the destined victim. He might possibly have respected, he would not have loved, her one whit the less for the deception. He went into Audrey's room after her maid left her, and his sister, on seeing him, hoped to be able to soften his anger, but for several minutes she found it impossible to get in a word. He walked up and down inveighing in the strongest terms against Laura, vowing at one moment that, of course, all was at an end between them; nothing would ever induce him to give his name and substance to such a combination of pride and defiance; the next, that he would appeal to her father,—she was not justified in refusing such an offer as his on her own responsibility. Mr. Erle ought to be told, and he would compel her to give up her absurd folly.

Audrey listened to his ravings with as much amazement as she had, in the early part of the day, listened to Laura's bitter sarcasms. She began to have serious doubts as to the expediency of a reconciliation.

The domestic hearth which would shelter two such firebrands would surely be in a perpetual state of combustion. She could only sit down and wait till the storm was over, and her brother had exhausted himself in a series of violent invectives. When he had grown a little calmer she gently suggested the impossibility of his wishing for an unwilling bride.

'I'd tame her,' he said fiercely, with a muttered oath. 'Besides, she wouldn't be unwilling. You know nothing at all about her. She isn't the milk-and-water you take her for!'

'But, Claude dear, you must know as well as I do that neither Mr. nor Mrs. Erle would attempt to force her into anything she disliked. They would think about it just as she does. Besides, she is of age.'

He was fully aware of all this, and when his passion cooled a little, admitted the uselessness of any appeal.

It had been arranged that he and Digby should start for Ireland the morning after the picnic. She begged him now to defer his journey, so that he might see Laura herself again.

He declined. There was no need, he said, that he should beg and entreat any woman to be his wife. Once refused, his offer would not be repeated.

'You will come in and say good-bye to me to-morrow before you go?' she asked.

'I always do, Audrey.'

'You are not angry with me about it, dear, are you?' putting her arms round him.

'I think you encouraged her in all this nonsense,' he answered gloomily; but he kissed her, and early the following morning came in to take leave of her.

'Let me give some message to Laura,' she

pleaded. 'Remember she did not refuse you at first, only on account of that condition, and, Claude, it did look like bargaining with her.'

'No; I will have nothing more to do with her.'

She drew his head down, and kissed him affectionately.

'Claude, it breaks my heart to see you go off unhappy and wretched. I had so looked forward to seeing you and Laura happy together.'

'You know whose door to lay it at,' he replied bitterly. 'She will go a long way before she finds any one willing to do as much for her as I would have done.'

Audrey was, no doubt, right in saying that neither Mr. nor Mrs. Erle would force Laura's inclination. They would not have done so, though they might seriously regret that anything should have occurred to interfere with a match so advantageous for her in every way.

But Laura resolved to spare them all

knowledge of the affair. Why should she add another to their many sorrows? Besides, telling them would involve an allusion to John's debts, a knowledge of which she was more than ever anxious to keep from them. She had actually written herself to the only two tradesmen whose names she could induce John to disclose, entreating their forbearance on the score of her father's delicate health, explaining that her brother was in daily expectation of some appointment, and promising faithfully that some portion, at least, of the debt should be discharged within the next six months.

Whether the simple appeal softened their hearts, or whether, as was most probable, they thought there was nothing to be gained by pressing their claims just then, both said they would wait a little longer.

But a fortnight of the six months was gone; every day was of importance; and she had not yet found a way of earning any money. She appealed in feverish anxiety to her friend.

'Audrey, do try to hear of some one wanting a governess; some one rich, I mean, not as poor as I am, because I want money, you see, not a home. I know I can teach, and I can play and sing. I hate singing before people, but I would do it if they would pay me.'

She had a splendid contralto, but could hardly ever be persuaded to use it except in church.

'Have you told any one you know of a governess?' she went on anxiously. 'I am twenty-two, and I think I look older, don't I? I would do my hair quite plainly—perhaps that would make a difference—only it will curl, so tiresome of it! Do you think I look too young to get a good salary?'

Audrey felt that her poor friend did look painfully young, but she remarked, in a consoling way, that one often saw such young and pretty governesses now that she could hardly conceive youth and beauty to be any drawbacks.

'They might think I would flirt,' said the

hapless Laura, with a dim consciousness of her besetting sin; 'but I wouldn't, indeed; I never want to speak to a man again. In fact, in one way, it would have been such a good thing if I had been a man myself; I could have got so much more money.'

'And spent it on yourself, or gone in debt, or married, or done something. You may be quite sure that if you had been a man, you would not have wanted to help your father to keep a curate.'

'No, I suppose I shouldn't,' coincided Laura, reflecting that her brother had shown no anxiety to lessen the family impecuniosity, 'and being a woman, I naturally think a woman the right thing. It was only about the money. It does seem hard that there are so few ways by which we can earn anything.'

What might have been the result had John honestly told Laura the real amount of his debts, it is impossible to say. He did not do so, and the thing she most dreaded happened.

A day or two after that conversation with Audrey, Mr. Erle received a letter at breakfast, saying that the writer, having in vain appealed to his son for payment of a long-standing debt, now addressed him, hoping there would be no farther delay in settling the bill. Enclosed was an account for 170*l*.

The letter dropped from Mr. Erle's hands, and he leaned back in his chair, pale and speechless.

John had not yet made his appearance. He was always late for breakfast—a fact which caused ceaseless discord between him and his father; but Laura and Mrs. Erle were present, and sprang simultaneously to the old man's side. Mrs. Erle dreaded some sudden seizure; her daughter too surely divined the real nature of the case.

Mr. Erle signed to his wife to read the letter; it was a shock to her, but nothing to the one she would have sustained had her husband been attacked by illness. His failing health was the great anxiety of her life; while he was well, or comparatively so, all other troubles were as a drop in the ocean. She spoke words of hope and comfort to him now.

It was wrong and foolish of John, but they would manage somehow, and when he got an appointment he would repay the money.

The mother's heart tried to find excuses for her son, but Mr. Erle would not be consoled. Debt was, in his eyes, disgrace. How could he hold up his head among his parishioners, or read from the altar, 'Thou shalt not steal,' while his son was possessed of goods for which he had not paid? He had from the pulpit always dwelt on the sin and folly of running in debt; now he would be pointed at as the preacher of truths he did not practise, or cause to be practised by his children.

He and John had never got on well together. The father resented the young man's idleness, his pleasure-loving habits. The son felt aggrieved at the old man's sternness.

A violent quarrel took place between them now. John stigmatised his father's notions about debt being 'disgraceful' as 'heroics,' while the latter inveighed against John's selfishness and extravagance. In his heart the young man bitterly repented his folly; he was weak, not vicious or unfeeling; but nervousness and extreme shame made him try to carry things off with a high hand. He told his father that so far from blaming him for running in debt he ought rather to congratulate himself on having so little to pay.

To his mother and sister, however, he spoke in a very different tone. They did not reproach him; what would have been the use? and to them he expressed deep contrition—sincere for the time, at least—and was prolific in promises for the future.

It needed all their skill to keep things smooth between him and Mr. Erle. The failing health of the latter gave way completely under the anxiety and the shock to his most cherished principles. Though living in a chronic state of quarrel with his son, he yet loved him with a tenderness almost womanly, and always suffered severely after a 'scene' with him.

These 'scenes' were of daily recurrence now, and tended still more to shatter the weak nerves and waning strength of the Rector.

For many weeks the household at Smedston Rectory was a sad one. Other bills came pouring in, for Mr. Erle had entreated his son to tell him all—to let him know the worst. When he knew all, he sat aghast. The payment would cripple him for the rest of his life.

How did not Laura thank God then that no anxiety respecting a trousseau for her was added to that heavy burden!

Mr. Erle had a small sum, the careful savings of years, invested for his wife, that she might not, at his death, be absolutely penniless. This sum he must now encroach on.

It barely sufficed to meet all the demands. They were met, and John Erle was a free man—but his father!

The whole thing had affected him to such an extent that he sank into a state of mental depression from which nothing could arouse him. He saw daily before his eyes his wife and pretty daughters dependents on the cold charity of the world.

It is a proverbial saying that pride and

poverty go hand in hand, and their pride is often enough made a reproach to the impecunious. Yet it is well that they should be proud. Their pride is their safeguard; it is, in fact, but another name for self-respect; and when self-respect dies it carries many other good qualities off with it.

The pride of the Erles made them conceal carefully this misfortune that had befallen them. Not one word was said of it to Mrs. Elliott, to Sir Digby Forester, to Audrey.

But the most carefully-guarded secret gets out somewhere or somehow, and there was no concealing Mr. Erle's illness.

The doctor who had known him for years told Mrs. Elliott and Sir Digby that only some great mental shock could thus suddenly have prostrated him. He was unable to take his duty; and a substitute being difficult of acquisition, the service had to be put off on two consecutive Sundays—once altogether, and once in the afternoon—as well as all the week-day services, to which, as a strict Anglican, Mr. Erle attached much value.

Little as he was to blame, he felt disgraced in his own eyes. The kindness and sympathy shown by every one overcame him, and when a neighbouring rector volunteered the good offices of his curate, and the stranger came to ask some trivial question, Mr. Erle broke down completely.

The medical opinion was that nothing but complete change of air and scene would restore him. Mrs. Erle's and Laura's hearts sank. How was he to get such change? The mere mention of it excited him violently. He had become suddenly possessed with a passion for saving, hoping that he might be enabled in some measure to replace the money he had destined for his wife. He would scarcely eat, would not touch wine or beer, and added to his own and his family's misery by catching a bad cold from sitting in his study without a fire.

Laura's proposal to leave her home and become a governess was the last drop of bitterness in his cup. When she first broached the subject he got very angry. He had not, he said, sunk so low as to be unable to support his daughter; to turn her, young and pretty, adrift among strangers. Then, when she gently urged the necessity of doing something, saying her mother did not disapprove, he buried his face in his hands and sobbed aloud.

In deep distress she knelt beside him, putting her arm round his bowed white head.

'Oh, don't, papa, don't; you kill me!' she exclaimed in an agonised voice.

By tender words and kisses she soothed him at last, promising to give up the scheme, as it so distressed him.

'No, my child,' he said, in a tone that went to her heart, 'do as you think best; I have no longer any right to dictate to you. I am a poor useless old man. But how can we —your mother and I—live without you? You are the light of our eyes—the one bright spot in our lives. Had you gone to a home of your own—but to be a governess! My beautiful little Laura! To be insulted, perhaps.'

'Insulted, papa? Who would insult me? The world is not quite so bad as that,' she said cheerfully. 'Besides, I can take care of myself; and even if any one did insult me, why, it wouldn't hurt me. Those sort of things don't really touch one; and as to my beauty'—laughing—'well, papa, you think a great deal of it—more than other people do; but it won't be any the worse if I earn a little money.'

She spoke cheerfully, but her soul was heavy within her. Trouble loomed on all sides, and her heart was always chanting a sad requiem for her lost love. She missed Claude daily, hourly. Whatever his faults he would have been kind and tender now. It was to her as if part of her life were taken away when day after day passed without tidings of him; without the messages which hitherto, during his absences, he had never failed to send through Audrey. She had no right to expect that it should be otherwise. But when was love ever reasonable?

CHAPTER XVI.

EVERY one at Enleigh was deeply concerned about Mr. Erle's illness, and all felt that it was probably as much mental as physical.

Audrey shrewdly suspected that John was in some way connected with it.

Sir Digby Forester, who was again the Dashwoods' guest, was exerting himself to the utmost to find something for the young man to do; but that was not an easy matter. Employment to suit him was not readily to be found, for John could handle a gun better than a pen, and train a dog better than cast up an account. He rode admirably to hounds— when he could get a horse—knew all the points of a dog, and would discourse scientifically on 'scent.' But, alas, he knew little else. His brains all lay in his hands and feet. He was born to be a pleasant kindly country gentleman; a keen sportsman; not a hard-working, self-denying bread-winner, and the constant association with the young men at Enleigh who, by the gift of fortune, were enabled to lead just the life that would have suited him, and with whom he shared that life to a great extent, for a mount and a gun and a dog were always at his disposal, had fostered his tastes, and made him less fit than ever for hard work.

Useless as he was to his family, he was yet a general favourite. There was something very lovable about his gay boyish manner; the *bonhomie* with which he got into scrapes, and the trusting confidence with which he appealed to any one at hand to get him out of them, and he was exceedingly affectionate, though he and his father were always at war.

Mr. Erle most unjustly reproached him because he was not as clever as Laura.

John reproached himself, too, with genial self-depreciation, but usually ended by reminding his progenitor that *he* was perhaps, on the whole, the person most to blame for his son's lack of brains.

'I've always thankfully accepted whatever gift Nature or any one else was good enough to bestow on me,' he would observe; 'and if you or she had given me brains, I should certainly have used them. Who knows? I might then have been a bishop! How ripping I should look as a bishop!' This was a sort of aside, and 'ripping' was Mr. John Erle's favourite expression. 'May a bishop hunt, Laura?'

His sister Laura among women, and Sir Digby Forester among men, were his ideals. During his boyish years he had worshipped the latter with a real honest hero-worship quite refreshing to see; and now, after the baronet's long absence, John was still his devoted admirer. And Sir Digby was very fond of him.

It had been no small trial to the young man to abstain from revealing to his hero the true source of the cloud which lay over his home; but though he was the exception to the pride which characterised his family, he had, out of deference to their repeatedly expressed wishes, abstained hitherto from any indiscreet revelations. As time went on, however, and he had the spectacle of his father's increasing weakness before his eyes, and as Laura persisted in her intention of leaving home, he found it impossible to avoid allusion to the subject in his intercourse with Sir Digby during the long days they spent together on the hill-side.

Had he been away from home, and not actually seen the consequences of his imprudence, his imagination would not have pictured them vividly enough to have distressed him; but the daily sight of his failing father, his mother, pale and composed, though consumed with feverish anxiety, his sister—the thought of Laura pained him beyond all else. The idea of her being a governess was insupportable to him. His was not the nature to realise that doing your part fearlessly and to the best of your power, however and wherever you can, is the one real stamp of nobility.

He was a slave to the world's estimate of people and things. Laura would lose caste if she earned money, for society has decreed that women may suffer, but may not, without forfeiting its favour, do anything to lessen that suffering.

That Laura scoffed at society and what it said on this matter, he attributed to her want of knowledge of the world.

His heart grew hot within him on the subject, and finally he spake with his tongue.

Audrey had had a letter from a friend, saying she wanted just such a governess as had been described in Laura, and begging that not a moment might be lost in securing such a treasure.

Laura was all eagerness to go, and John was in despair. He felt aggrieved with mankind at large for not intervening to prevent such a calamity. The idea did not occur to him of intervening in his own person by setting to work vigorously to find means of earning the money himself. Laura, in his case, would have driven a cab, or broken stones, or turned dog-trainer — anything rather than remain idle. Not so John. If somebody got him 'something to do,' he would do it, provided it was suited to him, and not too much trouble; but he had no thought of helping himself, and now he looked round, expecting some divinity in human shape to interpose between his sister and her quixotic scheme. But no divinity seemed at hand.

He and Digby had been shooting all the morning, and then sat down under a hedge on the breezy hill-side to lunch. For once the young man's appetite forsook him. In spite of his walk through the stubbles and his twenty-four years he could not eat.

Digby had noticed his depression, and at last, by kindly words and sympathetic looks, drew his secret from him. He confessed the whole thing with many expressions of contrition and denunciations of his own folly.

'Why in the name of fortune didn't you tell me at first?' said Digby. 'I would have helped you and saved all this trouble.'

'I asked Laura to speak to Miss Dashwood, but she wouldn't hear of such a thing,' he confessed fatuously.

'You should have come to me,' repeated Digby.

'If Laura would only give up this plan of hers!' said John.

Digby had never said much about that plan. John's objections to it had no weight whatever with him; he felt only increased admiration for her courage and energy; neither did he think her success doubtful, like Harold Carew. 'She is a plucky little thing, and will succeed in whatever she undertakes,' was his comment. But he doubted the Rectory machinery working without her, and he, besides, fully expected that the announcement of her resolve would be instantly followed by an offer of Claude's hand. 'Claude is a scoundrel if he doesn't make her such an offer,' was his mental conclusion.

Of all that had taken place he had, of course, no suspicion.

He had always been on terms of intimate friendship with the Erles, Mr. Erle having been his father's tutor, and entered most warmly into their troubles on this occasion; consulting eagerly with Audrey as to the best means of assisting them.

This was not an easy task, owing to their tenacious, sensitive pride.

With the exception of John, they held themselves haughtily aloof from anything like sympathy on the subject of that struggle for existence which they found so hard.

Intimate as they were, neither Audrey nor Mrs. Elliott had ever been able to persuade Laura to accept any little help in the way of dress, though that help had been proffered with scrupulous delicacy; for Mrs. Elliott, remorselessly unmindful of such weak things as feelings on some points, was yet full of appreciative generosity on others. She always did justice to the honest independence of the Erles.

'I honour them for it, my dear,' was her frequent remark to her niece.

Once, on the occasion of a grand ball at Enleigh, she had given both Audrey and Laura dresses and ornaments for the occasion, but she saw that the gift was, to the latter, more productive of pain than pleasure.

Laura could not receive a present with the facile grace by which some people make a donor feel that they have as much pleasure in accepting as he has in bestowing. Tears of sensitive pride rushed to her eyes. She could with difficulty be brought to take the dress, and she never wore it, as Mrs. Elliott plainly saw, without a secret feeling that she had forfeited, to a certain extent, her independence. This, it may be said, showed a want of real generosity. It would have been better to have accepted kindness in the spirit in which it was offered. That is true; but every one has the defects of his or her qualities, and a too tenacious pride was certainly the fault of all the Erles, John excepted. This it was which made it so difficult to help them. They could help Laura to a place as a governess, and John to a situation, if only one suitable to his capacities could be found; beyond this there was little that they could do.

There was another person deeply interested in the Erle family. That was Lady Emily Carew, who was excited by the news of their misfortunes in exact proportion to her gratitude to Laura and Mr. Erle for having saved her life, as she persisted in maintaining that they had, when it was menaced by 'those dreadful bulls.' She was as generous as the day, and ready to lavish kindness on, and receive it ungrudgingly from, every human creature. Her simple proposition now was to present Mr. Erle with the money he had paid for his son, so that he might re-invest it for his wife, and then to take him and her to Melbury for change of air and scene.

This proposition she disclosed to Mrs. Elliott and Audrey in great delight. Their assurances that it would be quite unacceptable to the Erles, that it would in fact be impossible to lay it before them, were alike surprising and unwelcome to her. She could not understand what objection there could be to the plan. She had more money than she knew what to do with. She had one son only, who had his own fortune quite independent of her. Melbury was hers for her life; her dear husband had always had a horror of the cruel custom which prevails in England of turning a widow out of the home in which her life has been passed just when her grief is fresh upon her; and as Melbury luckily was not entailed, he had left it to her entirely, to do as she liked with, only expressing a hope that she would leave it to Harold at her death.

'And indeed, my dears,' continued Lady Emily, 'he need not have troubled himself to express such a hope; for to whom should I leave it but to my darling son, who always lives there when he is not in London, or abroad, or somewhere else?'

All this and much more did Lady Emily confide to Digby and Audrey, dwelling further on the fact that she had 'no poor nieces or nephews, as so many people have, my dears; so nice for them, as then they can be kind to them; but I have no one; we are all rich and all only children, and Harold has all he wants,' in a regretful tone, as though Heaven had dealt hardly with her in depriving her of a son who stood in need of assistance.

What a boon John Erle would have been to her, had Fate decreed that she had been his parent! And now, when a benign Providence had thrown the Erle family in her way, what a manifest disregard of its designs did that singular race exhibit in rejecting her proffered help! She could scarcely be brought to believe in such perversity. She had evidently been 'raised up,' so to speak, in their behalf, and she felt that they were running counter to the wishes of the Almighty in thus showing themselves stiff-necked towards her.

It needed all Audrey's and Digby's influence to convince her that any offer to reimburse Mr. Erle, at present at least, would be unacceptable. Reluctantly she abandoned the idea. The visit to Melbury was a different thing. That seemed feasible, and Lady Emily secretly resolved to put the other part of her plan into execution at some future day.

CHAPTER XVII.

Laura Erle had to give up, for the time, at all events, her scheme of earning money as a governess.

When the preliminaries came to be arranged with that friend of Audrey's who was so laudably anxious to secure 'a treasure,' Mr. Erle sank into a state of hopeless depression, from which nothing could arouse him. He could not reconcile himself to the loss of his bright-faced child. The love of a father and daughter for each other, when both love their best, is the tenderest, as it is surely the most beautiful and ennobling, of all human affections. A daughter has a power of sympathy with her father's nature, because she shares it, which it is not given even to his wife to attain. From the day Laura could run alone and chatter to him in lisping accents, she had been the pride and joy of Mr. Erle's heart. He could have resigned her to a husband; that would have been natural and for her good, as he would have deemed; to part with her on any other terms was a trial greater than, in his weakened state, he could endure. The sight of his wife's grief added to his own. It is true she advocated Laura's going; not the less did she suffer in the prospect of losing her.

'My child, my child, how can I live without you!' was the agonised expression of her misery on the night when, in full family conclave, it was decided that Laura should go.

As has been said, the decision was not carried out. The doctor interposed. Presuming on the privilege of an old friend, he took upon himself to tell Laura privately that he could not answer for the consequences to her father if he was subjected to any further trial.

Reluctantly, therefore, after due consultation with her mother the scheme was abandoned. The money would have been of inexpressible value, but it would have been drawn, as so much of the money earned by women under present social arrangements is, from the life-blood of suffering human hearts.

'Thank you, my child; God will reward you for this!' was all Mr. Erle said when Laura told him she would stay at home; but his hand wandered caressingly over her head as she knelt beside him, and he spoke more that evening than he had done for weeks, though he seemed with difficulty to realise that he could keep his treasure. If she was for a moment out of his sight he inquired for her in an anxious distressed voice, as if fearing she would not return.

In all this there came one gleam of brightness. Lady Emily had taken up John's case, and by her indefatigable exertions had succeeded in getting him into a great banking-house, with one of the heads of which she was connected.

She certainly did not lose anything for want of asking, where her object was to serve a friend. She emulated the importunate widow with admirable results, refusing to take 'No' for an answer, agitating, writing, and making the lives of those unfortunates who had anything to bestow burdensome to them till she got what she wanted.

One evening she announced her intention of going up to town by the first morning train, saying she hoped to be back the following day, if not that same night.

She went and returned triumphant, having seen her cousin, and got John into the bank.

'I just went and caught him in his office, my dear,' she explained to Audrey, 'and told him he must do this for me. I had never asked him for anything before; and as he admired me very much in the days of my youth —for, indeed, I was pretty, my dear, though you would hardly believe it now—'

Audrey assured her she thought her beautiful at that moment.

'No, no,' with a shy laugh, and a perceptible blush on her charming old face; 'I'm not beautiful now, though my son says I'm a very nice old woman and not the least like a hag,' in which statement her son was, for once, quite right. 'But I was exceedingly pretty once, at least so my dear husband used to tell me, and this cousin too; so for sake's sake I told him he must do something for my young friend; and now, my dear, I think I'll go to bed, for, you see, I'm not so young as I was, and my maid is tired too, for she had not the same motive for exertion that I had, so felt the journey more.'

Lady Emily's very magnificent maid had not felt the journey at all, except as a pleasant diversion, but an object to love and take care of and 'fuss over' being necessary to her mistress's existence, Miss Scott had a good time of it, and she was hardly to be blamed if her poor head was just a little bit turned.

'You have quite taken the wind out of my sails, Lady Emily,' said Digby, as he got her candle; 'I was doing my best, but you have left me nowhere.'

She looked quite guilty.

'I never thought of that.'

He assured her laughingly how delighted he was to be thus anticipated, and, in truth, John Erle might have waited long for work before Sir Digby would have importuned his friends as Lady Emily did hers. He had the best intentions in the world, but he had some remains of moderation in his demands—some sense of the significance of a negative, which she had not.

'And now, my dear Mr. Erle, mind you are steady and work hard and all that, for I said all sorts of good things of you, so you must bear out my words; and some day I hope I shall see you a rich man like Whittington. "Turn again, Whittington, Lord Mayor of London Town," you know,' with an encouraging smile, which, if it had lost its youthful freshness, was yet beautiful as the reflex of the kindest heart that ever looked through human eyes.

John was both profuse and sincere, for the time, in his promises of exemplary conduct. He mentally commented thus: 'Fancy me

Lord Mayor of London! Ripping I should look, to be sure!'

What was to be expected from a young man who was perpetually picturing to himself his own 'ripping' appearance in certain distinguished but entirely imaginary positions?

The only expression of thanks Lady Emily would accept was a promise that Mr. and Mrs. Erle should visit her at Melbury immediately. They could not refuse. John's good fortune and the certainty that he should not lose Laura had brought back a gleam of hope to Mr. Erle. He became more amenable to wise counsel; was brought to see that starving himself, and sinking into utter despondency, and consequent uselessness, at Smedston was not the best way of helping his family; and consented to try what change of air and scene would do, though he uttered many doleful protests and laments respecting the expense of the journey.

John, his father better and Laura forced to give up her 'mad scheme,' felt his conscience quite at rest again, and started for his new work happily enough — as happily, that is, as was possible under the prospect of a long deprivation of hunting.

The day before he went, Lady Emily privately presented him with twenty pounds. Not being troubled with the family complaint, he willingly and thankfully accepted the gift; nor was it wonderful if he felt that he had been justified in expecting much from his friends, and in secretly cherishing the belief that, if he fell again, they would again pick him up.

Nevertheless, he honestly meant to keep the good resolutions he had made. Having disposed of John, Lady Emily's next care was to get Mr. and Mrs. Erle to Melbury with as little cost to themselves as possible. It was a long and expensive journey, and a curate had to be provided. The Dashwoods had few clerical belongings, but Digby bethought himself of a college friend, a clergyman at large, always ready, like a colonial bishop, for a stray duty, provided it were well away from his own appointed sphere.

This gentleman, who was much given to shooting, was most opportunely invited to Glynton, and he, on hearing the circumstances, immediately volunteered to take the Sunday services. Mr. Erle, who usually insisted on giving an equivalent for even ordinary acts of kindness, was with the greatest difficulty persuaded to accept his offer of gratuitous help, though money, the main consideration of the Rector's life, was, fortunately for himself, a matter of comparative indifference to the stranger.

Laura was to keep house during her parents' absence. The terrible trial of the last six weeks had somewhat diverted her mind from Claude; but now that the tension was lessened, the thought of him, her quarrel with him, her love for him, and the utter blank the complete break with him made in her life, came back with a painful force, which was redoubled by its compulsory banishment during that long interval.

The poor girl needed change little less than her parents. Terrible as the thought of leaving her home had been, she yet, to a certain extent, had looked forward to it as affording a relief from the torture of moving about amidst the scenes where she had been so happy with Claude. He was still in Ireland, and not one word of sympathy or remembrance did he send to her during those weeks of sorrow. Her heart asked wearily for some sign from him, but none came, and she longed with feverish longing for any absorbing occupation which would drown feeling.

Mr. and Mrs. Erle returned from Melbury, both much invigorated in health and spirits. John was going on steadily in London; Laura was safe under the paternal roof, not toiling as a governess among strangers; so things looked brighter altogether, had not a new and more terrible source of anxiety appeared. Laura drooped day by day perceptibly. To still that aching pain at her heart she worked incessantly, teaching both at home and in the schools; training the choir; visiting among the people—this last necessitating long and exhausting walks, owing to the straggling nature of the parish. In vain Audrey entreated her to moderate her exertions; in vain her parents interposed. She could only obtain in ceaseless activity any rest from mental suffering.

The village children noticed the change; the boys missed the bright vivacity which had delighted and civilised them, and to which they used to respond by broad smiles and surreptitious nudges of each other; the girls whispered among themselves that 'Miss Erle warn't well; she wur pale, and not so sperited-like.'

Claude's unkindness had struck a chill to her heart. He had been, in some sort, her ideal, an imperfect one, but still an ideal; and one does not lay one's ideals in their graves without many a pang over the brightness one lays down with them.

And during those weary months, when Laura had been mourning over his defection, he had been no less mindful of her. In the first paroxysm of his anger he had given Violet Ellis cause to think she might judiciously shorten line; but wrathful as he was, he could not bring himself to burn his bridges so completely as to cut himself off from all hope of reconciliation with that most obstinate and tormenting, yet fascinating, temptation at Smedston Rectory. He told himself again and again that she was cold, unnatural, strongminded, a designing flirt, a vile coquette; he did not trouble himself much about the compatibility of the various qualities he imputed to her; but in his secret heart he had to acknowledge that with all her faults and incongruities he would rather have her than the subservient Violet, eager to fling her pretty self at his head.

Sometimes he was tempted to surrender at discretion. Potent as this temptation was, however, he could not bring himself to be the first to lay down his arms, and he was not without hope that time would bring to her wisdom and humility.

As the dull winter months crept by, and she, lonely and miserable, contrasted the monotonous present with the future, which it was in his power to make so bright for her; as she saw her chances of matrimony disappear—Harold Carew had not renewed his visits to Enleigh—her proud spirit would surely be tamed, and she would respond gladly to the hand of reconciliation he would hold out.

But these hopes were suddenly dashed when he one day accidentally became aware that his fair adversary, less discreet apparently than Job's, or more daring, had not only written but actually printed a book. It cannot in truth be said that Mr. Dashwood felt the least disposition to take the said book on his shoulders, or bind it on him as a crown. He was furiously angry, and included Harold Carew, whom he considered chiefly to blame, in the maledictions which he freely uttered on the subject.

But if Laura chose to write, he could write too.

Anger, we have been told by various weighty authorities, is madness, and Claude was certainly mad for the time—beside himself with jealousy and wrath at the violation of all his most cherished prejudices by one he loved.

He heard, just at this moment too, that Laura was gone down to Melbury for a visit, which was likely to be of some duration.

In a paroxysm of fierce disgust and temporary hate he sought relief for his outraged feelings by the composition of a savage article on lady novelists for a periodical to which he contributed. Of this temperate and beautiful effusion Laura was the real theme. It certainly did more credit to his powers of scurrility than to his gentlemanlike feeling or his heart; but it relieved his over-wrought mood, and had he, having written it, burned it, all would have been well. He did not do so, however; and it remained a pleasing testimony to his calm judgment and large generosity of soul.

CHAPTER XVIII.

LAURA continued to droop more and more, and her mother, utterly at a loss to account for her depression, and deeply uneasy, had insisted on her accepting an invitation given by Lady Emily Carew.

The visit did not do her much good.

When well and happy she had derived immense amusement from Lady Emily and her ways. It was otherwise now that she was ill and depressed. She was too miserable to appreciate the curious mixture of strong common sense, childlike simplicity, unflinching moral courage, and abject physical fear which characterised her hostess.

Nor was this all. Lady Emily was deeply religious, in a lady-like way — that is, in her case, with a very decided reservation of perfectly well-bred and aristocratic worldliness. Her son was the great theme of her conversation. Once started on that congenial topic, she was supremely happy. Laura had only to listen.

The mother's feelings regarding this supreme object of her adoration were complex.

Her unbounded love for him was tinged with some awe, which had nothing of fear in it, and with an impatience almost amounting to contempt for some of his scholarly vagaries.

There were one or two points on which the young lady discovered that the mother and son were always at issue. The latter insisted on spelling his name Harald. This was a never-ending source of grief and annoyance to his parent. Not only was it unusual and incorrect, but it was a departure from the family tradition. There had been Harold Carews of Melbury for generations. His dear father, her husband, and his father before him, had been Harold Carew; and Lady Emily had always hoped to embrace a grandson who would bear that honoured name. But if it was to be changed into Harald for some 'literary quirk,' she would almost rather not see it perpetuated.

'And all my friends think it so odd, my dear; and no wonder! And they ask me why he does it; and then they set him down as eccentric.'

This was one grievance; another was the gentleman's heretical opinions respecting the sex. Having been blessed with such a mother as herself, Lady Emily could not but consider these opinions reprehensible and undutiful. What had she done that her only son should have acquired such notions about women? People would, of course, conclude that he generalised from his especial experience; and what a judgment must they not form of her! She felt personally reflected on and insulted by these views of his, not considering that in her son's eyes she was not a woman at all as other women are, but something quite apart —a being half divine, and with only some remaining attributes of womanhood about her, such as a disposition to scream when frightened, and a wish to provide him with a wife much against his will.

But all this could not amuse Laura now; it simply bored her. She hated the sound of Harold Carew's name, and even Lady Emily's abounding kindness was counterbalanced by her ceaseless loquacity on one subject. She found Melbury itself dull. The house lay in the valley, the downs rising before and behind, sheltering it from the winds, but also keeping off the free fresh air. A constant mist hung over the lake; the place was thick-strewed with dead and dying leaves. It was winter, not keen, bright, exhilarating, but damp, drizzling, depressing, the air saturated with moisture.

Laura, highly susceptible to all outward influences, suffered positive torture from utter depression of spirits. Day after day she rose with an increased inclination to suicide, asking herself hourly why it should be a duty to go on enduring life under conditions of such overpowering weariness. It seemed to her that the sun did not shine once during the whole of her visit.

When it did not actually rain, Lady Emily drove her in her pony-carriage to call on some of the people in the neighbourhood; people whom, of course, the girl did not know, and whose dull platitudes, to which she had to listen and reply, irritated her almost to madness.

Lady Emily never went up on the downs, the fresh air and the soft turf having a tendency to enliven her little steeds to the extent of making them start occasionally into something beyond the gentle trot dear to their mistress's heart and nerves; so they kept to the low-lying country, to the lanes, lovely in springtime and summer, but dank and dreary now, when the red mud lay ankle deep, and only a solitary leaf on some lonely branch remained to remind one of beauties passed away. Laura, accustomed to a hill country, where the winds made ceaseless music, and the cloud and mountain shadows an ever-shifting loveliness, found it terribly trying.

And the people they visited! There was a tall, extensive, fair, Juno-eyed Miss Bingley of Bingley Hall, destined by Lady Emily—as Laura gathered from various little remarks— to correct her son's views respecting the sex.

Miss Bingley, unimpassioned, fashionable, unexceptionably dressed, looked haughtily over the simply-attired, slight, girlish visitor, whose soul spoke in every look of her dark passionate eyes, addressing some careless questions to her: 'Had she been to the meet?' 'Did she know Lady Dash?'

The first positive feeling Miss Erle experienced after her arrival at Melbury was one of strong distaste for Miss Bingley's patronising airs.

Then there were Mr. and Miss Saffery, a bachelor and maiden brother and sister, who kept house together at Snail Farm.

Mr. Saffery was a clergyman by profession, but he had abandoned the cure of souls for that of insects and—hams. He farmed extensively, and made his pigs a very paying concern. In his leisure hours he devoted himself to entomology. His collection of beetles was famed through the country, and Laura was of course taken to see it. A new spectator was always a joy to Mr. Saffery. When the spectator had dark eyes, which went through him like an arrow,—above all, when she came from Melbury, with whose heir the entomologist had a standing controversy,—life had little better to offer.

A few days before her visit came to an end, Mr. Carew arrived at Melbury. His anticipated appearance threw his mother into a fever of joyful excitement. The servants, too, were all eagerly expectant; and from the remarks made, the young lady began to have some understanding of the adoration with which Lady Emily regarded him. It was evident that in his own home he must display qualities of a very different order from those which made him so unpopular in society.

He was shocked at the change in Laura. All her beautiful colour was gone. Her face had a delicate transparent hue, lovely in its way, but painful to see in her, because unnatural.

He had once accused her of being a termagant, of talking incessantly. She was no longer open to such a charge; she sat still and silent, never volunteering a word; and when she did speak in reply to a question, it was without any of the flippancy which he had found so reprehensible.

'Whose doing is that?' he asked his mother. 'Is it Dashwood's?'

Lady Emily did not know. It was, she thought, anxiety about her father and brother. 'Forester said something about a marriage between her and Claude Dashwood.' The lady had not heard anything; though she had certainly noticed that Claude had seemed very attentive to his sister's pretty friend; but as nothing had been said to her on the subject, she had avoided any allusion to it.

'Well, between them they have pretty well taken all the spirit out of her.'

It would have been well had he, in his intercourse with his mother's young guest, imitated his mother's reticence; but tact was not Mr. Carew's strong point. If it was possible to blunder into an awkward topic, he was sure to do so. He never entered into conversation with Laura without dragging in Claude Dashwood's name. It almost seemed as if there was some fascination in it for him; and as she could not hear it without a vivid and painful blush, and was unable to speak of Claude without a suffocating sense of misery, she absolutely dreaded the sight of her host, kind as he tried to be to her.

Had she been well and bright, as when first he knew her, he might have avoided her; but her delicate drooping appearance touched some tender fibre in his heart, making his manner particularly gentle to her.

In his own home he came out in a totally new light. To his mother, especially, he was so winning and affectionate that her partiality was more than justified. He had the good taste not to be demonstrative in public, but Laura's presence did not wholly prevent his showing Lady Emily a thousand little attentions—talking to and laughing with her, teasing her good-humouredly from time to time, and then apologising in a half-tender, half-caustic way, very characteristic.

The day before Laura was to return home she was standing disconsolately enough at the front door, watching the mist driving down the valley, wishing it would either rain decidedly or clear up, so that she could go out. As she stood, Harold, followed by a brace of dogs, came up.

'Have you been on the hill to-day, Miss Erle?'

'I have never been on it.'

'Never? Do you mean to say you haven't been on the Encampment?'

'No; the weather has been so bad.'

'But it is beautiful up there. I have just come down. You have no idea how pleasant it is. Will you come up? It would do you good.'

'I should so like it.'

'Come then, will you?'

'I will get my cloak, and tell Lady Emily.'

'Your cloak by all means, but never mind Lady Emily. She is down at the Lodge talking to Mrs. Fay; and if she misses you she will suspect where I have taken you.'

'Is the hill your favourite resort?'

'I never miss going there when I'm at Melbury. On a clear day you can see the Isle of Wight from the top,' taking her cloak from her. It was the same red one he had once seen Claude wrap so carefully round her.

'Pray don't trouble,' she said, trying to take it from him; 'I always carry my cloak myself.'

'Not always, surely. I have often seen Claude Dashwood carry it for you. Besides, you don't look fit to carry it or anything now,' with a compassionate glance.

The bracing air as they went up the hill was fresh life to her. They got above the mists; the clouds broke, and streaks of blue showed themselves through the curtain of gray that had obscured the sky down in the valley. Her eyes brightened, and a shade of colour returned to her face.

'How delightful it is!' she exclaimed, with something of her old vivacity. 'I must have my cloak; it is much colder up here!'

He attempted to put it round her, but she declined his offer, taking it from him and putting it on herself. No man but Claude had ever assisted her with it; he had a way of his own of doing it—throwing it over her shoulder so as to make her look 'like an Irish girl,' as he said. She could not bear the thought that any one else should do it now. She had quarrelled with him, and he was lost to her; but she could not so soon put away his memory, and let another take his office.

Harold was disappointed. He had wished to put her cloak on for her. It was associated in his mind with the first day he had seen her, when she had 'quarrelled with and snubbed' him all the morning, made him laugh in spite of himself at dinner, and then come back to him in the moonlight the impersonation of girlish coquetry, with that cloak round her, her hat tilted down over her eyes, to shake hands with him as he stood on the steps.

That picture was constantly recurring to his mind; but with it came the image of Claude, looking on and waiting for her as one who had a right to wait, and to be impatient if she stayed too long. The second picture neutralised the pleasure the first gave him. He would like to have put her cloak on; why, he could hardly say, unless it were to show himself a foe to monopolies.

Laura did not wear her cloak picturesquely now, as if Claude had put it on. She threw it simply and soberly round her, as became one from whose life the bright lights had passed away.

'The air has done you good,' said Harold. 'I knew it would. You ought to have come here every day; it would have brought back your colour. When first I saw you, you were as red as a rose; now you are as pale as a lily.'

This poetic flight from the lips of her former antagonist took Laura quite by surprise.

'There, you are not pale now,' he went on, as the blood rushed to her face, partly from amusement, but chiefly from embarrassment at the allusion to old days.

Unfortunately Laura did not know that the encampment on the hill was the subject of a standing controversy between her learned host and that bachelor hunter after beetles—Mr. Saffery.

The latter gentleman had a theory of his own about it. He maintained that it was the grave of Hector—his 'tumulus,' he called it. It may be said at once that language quite failed to express Mr. Carew's profound contempt for this belief. That any sane man should entertain it, was to him so astounding that his wonder at it never grew less. It went on increasing till it culminated in a sort of amazed incredulity—'Saffery couldn't really believe it!'

Had Miss Erle been better acquainted with Mr. Carew, she would no more have trusted herself alone on the hill with him than she would have flown.

She would have known how inevitable it was that the whole case, Carew *versus* Saffery, should have been gone through for her benefit; but she did not know, and suffered herself to be led towards the disputed points, all unconscious of her doom.

Mr. Saffery had lately been ill-advised enough to lecture to a local audience on the 'Tumulus of Hector;' and in that lecture he had, while professing the profoundest respect for his adversary personally, made short work, in his own estimation, of his adversary's theories, so subversive of his own.

Mr. Carew despised a lecturer above all living creatures. He described him as 'a fool standing behind a table talking to other fools in front of the table;' but in this instance he was almost tempted to play the fool himself, and give a counter lecture, in which Mr. Saffery, for whom he professed no respect whatever—how could he respect a man who believed that Hector was buried on the top of a hill in ——shire?—would be made to undergo some potent blows from the hammer of

Truth and Common Sense, wielded with right good will by the scholarly heir to Melbury.

However, on reflection, he would not degrade himself by such a proceeding.

As John Erle would have said, 'he couldn't fancy himself' delivering a lecture; so Saffery remained master of the situation.

But the pleasure of having a listener—albeit a soulless woman-creature—to his refutation of these monstrous fallacies was not to be resisted, and Laura, almost before she was aware of it, found herself in the thick of the controversy.

From point to point he drew her on, going still higher and higher, till they had nearly reached the top. And as they ascended his eloquence increased. It culminated in an appeal to his companion—

'Is it conceivable that a sane man should hold such a theory, or find any one to accept it?'

'Certainly not,' responded Laura, who was getting very tired; 'I should say he was insane, and his followers too.'

Harold was delighted.

Clearly there was something quite above the average in this girl. Adversity, whatever may have been its nature, had brought out some gleams of reason in her; and if he was tempted to regret for a moment that vivacity which had impressed itself pleasurably on his memory, was not the deficiency more than compensated for by the gain in insight and appreciation of real scholarly worth which her explanation of Mr. Saffery's beliefs implied?

It was even to be regretted that she was going away the next day. What further improvement might not a more prolonged intercourse with a superior mind effect in her?

Long before they got to the bottom of the hill again a heavy shower came on, such a shower as comes only on the open downs—pelting, driving, pitiless rain, that chills you through and through. The wind blew as if it were coming from all four quarters of the heavens at once, and meeting up there for a wild dance of its own. It almost lifted Laura off her feet.

'Will you take my arm? You had better,' said Mr. Saffery's opponent.

No. Miss Erle preferred being independent. The excitement of battling with the wind had taken off her fatigue, and she looked as red and fresh as a rose dripping with dew when they reached Melbury, both wet through.

Lady Emily scolded her son volubly for having exposed Laura to such a risk.

'It is enough to kill her.'

Mr. Carew looked deeply compunctious. It would be a serious thing to kill a creature capable of solving inexplicable questions by common-sense solutions. His compunction at the mere contemplation of such a catastrophe was almost enough to justify Claude's uneasiness.

CHAPTER XIX.

To Miss Erle's extreme surprise, Mr. Carew, on bidding her 'good-night,' informed her of his intention of accompanying her on the first part of her journey on the following day.

She had to change trains twice. At one place she would have to wait at a small inconvenient station; at another she had to cross the line, having only a very short time to do it.

Laura protested. She was quite capable of taking care of herself, and in secret felt much bored at the prospect of Mr. Carew's company.

She had hardly spirit left to be amused at his venturing to trust himself alone with her. A passing feeling of wonder—'Does he think me so far beneath him as not to be dangerous?'—did occur to her, but it made no impression. She cared too little about him to waste thought on him.

'I wish you would not trouble. How bored you will be!' she had said to him in her first moment of surprise.

'Why should you say so?' he remonstrated. 'I like to go with you; and I am sure you are not equal to the exertion of looking after your luggage.'

Miss Erle's luggage was of too modest a nature to need much care on any one's part.

With many tender farewells Lady Emily left her at the station, her kind eyes full of tears. Laura's visit had made her long more than ever for a daughter.

But she would ask 'dear Miss Bingley' to Melbury. She was such a charming girl, and dear Harold liked her—negatively, that is. He did not positively object to her. She did not talk much—a great recommendation; and then, what she did say was always said with propriety.

Laura felt very ungrateful. Lady Emily

and her son had overwhelmed her with kindness. The latter had been a marvel of gentle courtesy to her; yet he wearied her to death. She had no inclination whatever to convert him now, or to quarrel with him. Even speaking was an exertion to her. He soon perceived this, and abandoned all attempts at conversation; but at the first large station he bought some newspapers and magazines, which he gave to her, saying they might amuse her.

One of the first things she saw was that admirable composition in which her late lover had relieved his feelings. She was well acquainted with his style, and knew the periodicals through which he was in the habit of imparting his ideas to the public. She had no doubt whatever that the paper in question was his, and that he had taken her as his text. She read it through, at first with profound amazement, which changed into contemptuous disappointment in him as she went on. She had never conceived it possible he could stoop to use such weapons.

'That is the sort of revenge he finds comfort in,' was her mental comment. 'I hope he feels the better for it.'

She was no longer pale and languid, and Mr. Carew, who seemed to derive much instruction or amusement from watching her furtively, was puzzled to account for her sudden change of expression and bearing. He was more than ever convinced that woman was a mystery too deep for the mind of man to fathom. He did not leave her till the change of train had been effected, and he saw her comfortably settled in a through carriage; then he said good-bye, feeling again that vague sense of disappointment which he had experienced on the hill when she refused to let him put on her cloak. He had been sensible of some pleasurable excitement at the prospect of travelling with her. He liked to look at her; she stimulated his curiosity; and her behaviour on this occasion roused that curiosity to the highest pitch. But it would have been more satisfactory had she seemed to be aware of his presence or conscious of his efforts to amuse and interest her. It is of little use being attentive to a charming young lady if she continues quite insensible to your exertions, and does not seem to know or care that she is a subject of interest to you.

Claude had never been home since his quarrel with Laura. He prolonged his visit to Ireland far beyond the duration first assigned to it, and then went to London. But at Christmas he could not avoid coming down, for Charlie Dashwood was to be at home, and his brother could not have absented himself without giving rise to much comment, necessitating awkward explanations.

Besides, Claude did not wish to absent himself. He had undergone tortures of jealousy from the moment he had learned that Laura had gone to Melbury. Every other sentiment gave way to the one passionate resolve to keep her from Harold Carew. And he must see her. Nothing else would stop that maddening restlessness which tormented him night and day.

Enleigh was to be full of people at Christmas; he came down, therefore, a week before, hoping to see her quietly.

He had not exactly made up his mind what to do. He would see her. That was the great thing. He did so at church on Sunday morning, having only arrived late on Saturday night.

Even the flush which always dyed her face with beauty at his coming could not conceal from him the change in her appearance. He was deeply shocked—physical suffering always affected him—and, for the first time, a sudden flood of remorse for his hardness to her came over him. But he would see her now and compensate her for all her sufferings.

He waited outside the church door, thinking she would follow after finishing the voluntary. Instead, she joined her father in the vestry, and went thence through a side-door leading into the rectory garden; so Claude waited in vain.

'How shockingly ill Laura looks!' he said

to Audrey. 'You did not tell me how bad she was.'

'You have much to answer for,' was her reply.

He turned away with a vague feeling of uneasiness. He had not been without a consciousness that she might have suffered a good deal, but the consciousness had not been disagreeable to him. He hoped that the suffering would 'tame her,' and he had suffered so much himself that autumn through her that he could not entirely regret her share of the probation. But then, in the case of a pretty woman, suffering should never go beyond the point at which looks may be affected. Laura had certainly grown too thin.

He walked down to the church again in the afternoon, hoping to catch her as she came out. She again avoided him, nor were any further efforts he made more successful.

He did not want to send her a formal message; he would rather have met her as if casually somewhere.

When Tuesday came, and he had not seen her, he said to his sister,

'Does Laura never come here now?'

'Yes, sometimes.'

'I should like to see her, Audrey.'

'Well, go and call on her. I don't think she is likely to come here just at present,' dryly.

'You mean that she doesn't want to see me. Has she said anything about my coming?'

'She has not spoken of you at all.'

When Audrey was angry some portion of Mrs. Elliott's sarcastic trenchant manner seemed to pass into her. Claude, highly sensitive, felt her tone and was hurt. Men always do feel hurt at the least sign of resentment in a woman, no matter what they have done themselves.

'Audrey, don't speak in that way,' he remonstrated, with mingled impatience and reproach. 'You know the—the interest I take in Laura; our having quarrelled does not prevent my being sorry to see her looking so ill. Have you heard how she is to-day?'

'I have not, Claude; I haven't seen her since Sunday.'

He walked to the end of the room and back; he always walked about when he was nervous—a reprehensible habit some persons have, jarring to the nerves of sensitive people, especially if the pedestrian happen to be built on a large scale; then he sat down by the writing-table for a minute, got up again for another turn, and finally subsided with his back to the fire, one foot on the fender and an expression of gloomy discontent and injured feeling on his handsome face.

Audrey's ball of wool fell off her lap and rolled close to his feet. He picked it up, and carrying it across the room to her, said,

'Tell me about her, Audrey,' in a tone of imperious entreaty.

'Excuse me, Claude; I have nothing to tell.'

'You certainly don't treat me with much sisterly confidence,' he said bitterly.

'One learns by experience. The wisdom of the serpent is not less necessary to enable one to get through life than the harmlessness of the dove. You forget that you have taught me how my confidence may be received.'

'Because one is angry about a thing once it does not follow that one is to be so always.'

'It follows, nevertheless, that one judges of what is likely to be by what has been.'

'What do you mean?'

'I mean now that I will not talk to you about Laura.'

'Then I think that you are very unkind;' with which boyish expression of annoyance Mr. Dashwood strode to the writing-table, and did this time begin to write.

He felt more surprised and hurt than he had ever been before in his life. Anything like implacability was, he would have said, entirely foreign to the nature of his sister or her friend. Both had hasty tempers, but their anger was soon over, and Laura especially—excitable, but affectionate and generous—was won by the least show of kindness. He was debating as to whether he had not better call on Laura, when, as he was lying that afternoon on the sofa in his sister's boudoir, the subject of his thoughts came suddenly into the room. It is needless to say that she had not expected to find him there. She was under the impression that he had gone out riding.

He started up.

'Laura! at last! I have been so anxious to see you,' holding out his hand warmly. 'I am grieved to find you looking—not well.'

The warmth of his greeting took her completely by surprise.

'Do you mean to say you won't shake hands with me?' in a tone of pained amazement, as she did not take the one he proffered.

Laura had made a thousand vows that she would never again touch the tip of Claude Dashwood's finger; but, all vows notwithstanding, she did not find it an easy matter to decline shaking hands with a person who was standing before her requesting her to do so, more especially as the wrong she was resenting was one personal to herself. Had she been resenting Audrey's grievances, she might have found it less difficult to keep her resolutions. As she was resenting her own, she broke them, not willingly, however, for she gave her hand as coldly and reluctantly as it was possible to give it. He tried to retain it.

'You have been ill—anxious. You look pale. I was so sorry,' nervously.

She withdrew her hand haughtily.

'I was anxious about papa—we all were; that was all, thank you.'

She turned to speak to Audrey respecting the parish matters about which she had come, and then with a bow was leaving the room. On seeing her about to go, Claude interposed—

'Don't go, Laura. I have been wanting to see you. I—'

Even in old days she had always resented his assumption that when he wanted to see her she was to come to him. Had he been anxious to see her now, why had he not called?

'I am sorry I cannot wait,' she interrupted coldly. 'I am very busy, and only came to speak to Audrey for one moment. I thought you were alone, Audrey,' with a significant glance at her friend.

She quitted the room in a paroxysm of anger. What did his reception mean? Did he look on her as a fool, or a plaything to be taken up and flung down at his pleasure?

She left the house, and went out into the park, anywhere to be alone. She had been going to the village, but felt she could not do so now. To the young, every new sensation in themselves, every fresh revelation of character in those around them, is a discovery; and when the discovery is of a painful nature, the soul, inexperienced in suffering, shrinks with horror at the contemplation of hitherto unsuspected evils.

Laura did not know to what she was to attribute Claude's conduct. Had he, then, never been open and trustworthy? She was alarmed, too, at the storm of passionate anger that swept over herself. The better part of her was, for the time, powerless before it.

Almost mechanically she had directed her steps towards the encampment—Enleigh, too, could boast of such a fruitful source of discord—and sat down on the root of an ash-tree under which she and Claude had often rested.

How long she sat she did not know. A sudden sense of all she had to do and ought to be doing came upon her, and she started up. As she did so, she found herself face to face with Harold Carew.

It must be explained that he and his mother had arrived at Enleigh on the preceding day, anticipating their expected arrival by twenty-four hours.

Mrs. Elliott had asked them down in furtherance of her own scheme of counteracting Claude's intentions respecting Laura.

Harold had come hither now to make some calculation about the encampment, a great source of interest to him always, not certainly expecting to find any one there, least of all Laura.

Both looked embarrassed at this unlooked-for meeting, the gentleman feeling guilty in some way, as people do who have suddenly intruded, however unwillingly, on the sorrows of others; for the traces of tears in Laura's eyes, the expression of pitiful misery on her face, told their own tale.

A man less simple or more accustomed to women would have spoken to her as if unconscious that anything was amiss; but of that sort of ready tact he was quite devoid, and he showed plainly the concern he felt. His look of distress restored her self-possession.

'Have you come up to see the camp, Mr. Carew?' she said. 'We cannot boast of such a one as you have at Melbury.'

'I—I beg your pardon; I'm afraid I disturbed you,' in tones of blundering kind-heartedness. 'I'm going away again.'

'Pray don't on my account. I was just going myself. I came up here to—for the sake of the air. I took it on my way to the village.'

'Won't you allow me to go with you?—to see you home?' he asked, as if uncertain whether he ought to offer to accompany her or not.

'No, thanks. I am going to the village for papa; I always go alone.'

'Let me, at least, open the gate for you.'

They walked on in silence, he looking infinitely distressed. He could no more bear to see a woman suffer than a dumb animal. Both were unable to defend themselves; for though women were certainly not dumb, yet, being unreasoning and unreasonable creatures, they stood, owing to their natural infirmities, even more in need of protection than birds or quadrupeds.

When they reached the gate he spoke:

'Why do you cry?' he asked, with the abrupt bluntness of a schoolboy. 'Are you unhappy? What is it? There are tears on your eyelashes now. Can I—could my mother do anything for you?'

For a moment surprise kept her silent; then she answered gravely,

'Mr. Carew, have you ever been very, very angry about anything?'

'Angry?' hesitating. 'Well, yes, I suppose I have. I don't often get angry, but I do sometimes,' in an exculpatory voice.

'Well, and what do you do?'

'Do? I—I don't know exactly. What do you mean?'

'What do you do to relieve your feelings?'

'I don't know exactly,' looking puzzled and wondering if she thought he relieved them by tears.

She looked at him with one of her old smiles.

'You swear sometimes, just a little, don't you? Most men do; I mean, at least, all the men I know, except papa.'

He looked convicted.

'I don't say I have never done such a thing.'

'Well, tears in a woman correspond to swearing in a man. They let off the steam.

Where a man swears a woman cries; and you must think no more of having seen me in tears than I should if I happened to hear you use some rather strong language.'

'I should not swear before you, I hope.'

'Nor did I mean to let you see me crying. I was very angry, that was all.'

'But can I help you?'

'Yes; say nothing about having seen me in tears. In fact, forget that you met me here at all.'

'I cannot promise that, but I will not speak of it.'

'Thank you; your kindness has been of more use than perhaps you can ever know,' with an honest simple look of gratefulness. 'Now we will go on our way, each of us. Good-bye,' holding out her hand.

They parted, he keeping the gate open for her and taking off his hat as she passed through, then following her with his eyes as she went down the steep encampment.

His words of sympathy had come to her like a spar to which she could cling in the sea of angry emotion on which she had been tossed.

Claude's conduct had shaken for the moment her belief in truth and goodness; but her anger was now calmed, and her self-control resumed its sway. Harold's few words of unaffected genuine kindness soothed her wounded feeling to a degree out of all proportion to their apparent significance. It was that they spoke to her better nature, enabling it to regain its ascendency at a time of bitter conflict.

From another bit of rising ground in the park a gentleman had been watching the two as they walked together and then stood still at the gate for that last little colloquy.

When Laura left Audrey's room, Claude had sat down again on the sofa, surprised and angry at her reception of his cordial greeting. For months he had been pining for one word from her, for one touch of her hand, one smile from her. He had been too proud to seek her, but was ready and willing to be gracious when he could be so without any compromise of his dignity. And then to have the cup snatched from his lips, and no compunction shown in the snatching of it! He had not expected that she would have given in all at once, thrown herself metaphorically into his arms *à la* Violet; but there was a calm determined haughtiness in her manner which alarmed him, and which he had not expected. There was no longer the girlish defiance which had made her refuse his assistance at the stile, and which was, little as she knew it, a most delicate tribute to his influence over her. He could not flatter himself there was any such tribute in her manner to-day.

He left his sister's room, and went out into the park. There he saw Harold going towards the encampment, and afterwards, when he reached the ash-tree, Laura rise up as if to meet him.

With jealous eyes he watched them walk towards the gate, stand, talk, and then part as if lingeringly.

He felt almost beside himself. This, then, was the reason she would not stay to speak to him. She had appointed to meet his rival there. She had not been long in supplying his place. But Carew should never have her! She had been his before that combination of pedantry and priggism had ever seen her, and he would not yield her up to him now. Even if he could not have her for himself, he would not suffer her to fall into another's hands. Such was his fierce resolve at that moment.

He had gone out with some vague idea of meeting her on her way back from the village, and this was what was in store for him!

END OF VOL. I.

LONDON:
RODSON AND SONS, PRINTERS, PANCRAS ROAD, N.W.

www.ingramcontent.com/pod-product-compliance
Lightning Source LLC
Chambersburg PA
CBHW032116230426
43672CB00009B/1761